Perspectives of Kingston-on-Soar

Compiled by

Brian and Veronika Smith

'Memories for the Millennium'

by the

*Nottinghamshire Living History Archive
Millennium Award Scheme*

Published by the "Nottinghamshire Living History Archive Millennium Award Scheme"

ISBN 1-904102-24-7

Copies of this book are made available through the Nottinghamshire County Libraries and the Nottingham City Libraries. This publication contains extracts from oral history interviews; full transcripts and audio recordings of these Interviews are also available at selected libraries. Copies of the book may be available to purchase from the author. Please contact the Local Studies Department of the Central Library, Angel Row, Nottingham, NG1 6HP for further details.

Whilst every care has been taken to ensure the accuracy of the information contained in this publication, Nottinghamshire Living History Archive Millennium Award Scheme cannot accept any responsibility for any error or omission. Attempts have been made to contact copyright holders where appropriate. If any have been inadvertently missed out, this will be rectified in future editions.

© Brian & Veronika Smith 2002. All rights reserved

Printed by
Technical Print Services Ltd, Nottingham, England.

Foreword by Lord Belper

I am pleased to give my support to this new book on Kingston-on-Soar.

My family have played a major part in the affairs of the village since they came here in 1845, notably the erection of a school and village hall, and the rebuilding of St. Winifred's Church.

Many memories of the village have been recorded, and many new photographs have come to light. I myself remember visits to the well loved Kingston Show as a boy.

The recollections of changing life in Kingston make a valuable contribution to Notts. Local History, and I am sure this book will give much pleasure and interest to future generations.

Belper

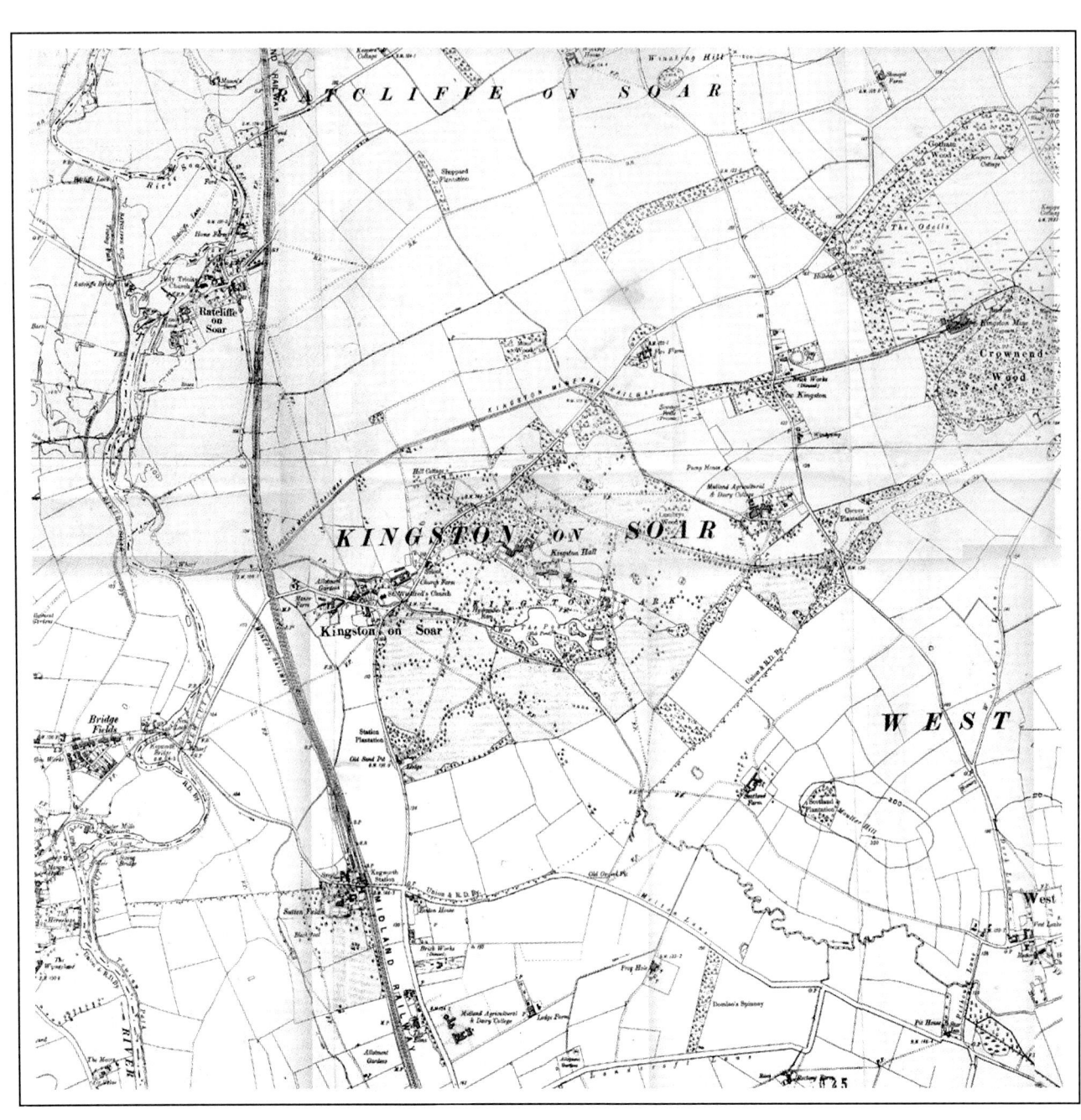

Reproduced from the 1921 Ordnance Survey map

Contents

Introduction	1
1. Kingston Hall	2
2. Lady Belper's School	10
3. Kingston Gypsum Mine	18
4. The Gypsum Railway	24
5. Farming & Agriculture	28
6. Shooting Days	36
7. The Midland Agricultural & Dairy College	40
8. The Fine Art Company	44
9. Skating on the Lake	46
10. World War II Years	50
11. Kingston Show	58
12. Village Shops & Trades	66
13. Village Life	70
14. Washdays	76
15. Floods	78
16. Social Life	82
17. Down by the Riverside	86
Interviewees	88
Acknowledgements	91

Cover photo: The Hon. Ronald Strutt (late 4th Lord Belper) Coming of Age celebration. Kingston Hall 9th June 1933

Introduction

The recording of oral history has grown apace since the pioneering work of George Ewart Evans, who, in the early 1950s, chronicled the memories of East Anglian country folk.

In older societies, information passed from grandparents to grandchildren was of great importance for obvious reasons. The elders were the sole carriers of the tradition. In modern society the older generation has largely lost this role, yet their memories of their community and family are still of great value in recording the changes in the social history and working conditions of that community. They help knit together its identity.

The estate village of Kingston-on-Soar, lying on the south-west border of Nottinghamshire, has had a fairly stable existence since the arrival of the Strutt family in the mid-19th century. However, as in most villages, agriculture, industry, estate life, village life in general, has gone through much change in recent times.

We have attempted to document Kingston's past within living memory – before the changes in and around the village had taken place – and give a glimpse into ways of life that have either changed forever, or disappeared.

This book is based largely on recorded interviews with residents, ex-residents, people who worked in Kingston, together with some who were visitors to the village. The stories and perspectives are entirely those of the interviewees.

We are grateful to every person who gave their time, and shared their memories and knowledge for this project.

Brian & Veronika Smith.   March 2002

Kingston Hall

'a truly impressive place'

The Elizabethan style Hall was built for the Strutt family by Edward Blore in 1842. Edward Strutt, MP, took up residence in 1845. He was created Baron Belper in 1856. Kingston Hall remained home to this branch of the family until 1977 when it was sold by Ronald, 4th Lord Belper.

'**My** father [Algernon Henry, 3rd Lord Belper, 1883-1956] was quite an elderly father, because he'd been married before. I think he was thirty-seven when he married my mother. He did a lot of good work in Nottinghamshire. He worked for the County Council and did many other things during the war, but he was too old to be on active service. I enjoyed his company very much. He was a very nice person to be with. My mother [Lady Angela Belper, 1901-1995] she was great fun, but we had to rather watch our 'P's and 'Q's with her. She kept us well in hand … and on the straight and narrow path. We were very fond of our parents.'

'I had a very happy boyhood, my parents were very good to me. But also somebody who loomed very large in my life was my nanny Patty Dolman, who used to live in the Lodge gatehouse on her retirement. I saw quite a lot of her because my parents were great travellers. They used to go all over the world, Canada, S. Africa, New Zealand and

Lord & Lady Belper with Lavinia and Rupert, 1926.

my father was very keen on fishing and deer stalking and that sort of thing. Therefore I was with my nanny quite a lot. I was very fond of her.'

'They did a lot for the village, particularly my mother. She was very much liked in the village, very popular I think. She had a great sense of humour and she was a great one for practical jokes.'

(The Hon. Peter Strutt)

Nanny Dolman (nee Smith) and Peter Strutt, Kingston Hall, 1926.

'**Algernon** Henry Strutt, he was a very upright, aristocratic man. He was a real gentleman. I got on very well with him and the family, because he was the Lord Belper that was here when we first came.'

' He was a great benefactor to the parish. It was a feudal village in those days, because the Belper's were head of everything. It didn't matter whether it was the church or the Village Hall. Anything that was run, was all run by the Belpers as the head, and they asked people to help and so forth. They found the incentive and the ideas and then sold it to the parishioners, and everybody buckled in. But, yes they were very good. But after they'd gone it was changed somewhat because the feudal system really disappeared.'

' He would come in [to Church Farm] without a doubt. If he wanted you he would come down in his car, sit on the road and blow his horn until someone appeared. Which is one way of getting people out.'

(Norman Beeby)

'**Well,** Lord and Lady Belper they were fine Lord and Lady they was. They used to come down into the village and go round the people's houses; they'd stop and have a cup of tea; they'd have a chat with you. They didn't exactly show their position to what they was against the village people. They was as you might say Mr and Mrs Belper as far as we was concerned in the village. That's how they used to come talking to you. As a Lord and Lady they probably - when they had their parties and the people of the same class come to Kingston Hall - they used to show it then. But as far as the village [was concerned] the Lord and Lady were two of a kind with the village people.'

(George Vickers)

'**The** Third Lord Belper I remember later on, when I was a teenager. A very nice gentleman. He was good to his men because when he died he left them all some money.
' I was very fond of Lady Belper, she was very good to me. She sometimes used to tell me to come up and she'll pass some dresses on to me. Lovely dresses they were too – she was very kind.'

(Sylvia Church nee Joyce)

'**Lady** Angela, she was quite a card really. Liked her own way as well.
 But she was good, very good, in the village. To some of the older ones – if they were ill – she would take soup and things like that. They really – in those days – they treated all the villagers like their family, which today seems to have disappeared.'

(Mary Beeby)

'**Very** nice lady. I always said you could say she was a real lady. My mother was very ill, I can't just remember the year, but she had a erisipelas. Mrs Daykin used to come in and give me a hand 'cos she had to have a mask on because her face was so sore - this black ointment put on it. So Mrs Daykin made me a mask with like a gauze thing put on. And apart from Mrs Daykin, Lady Belper was the only person who went to see my mother while she was in bed. She was in bed for nearly a fortnight. Then she had a relapse and was a few weeks again. Lady Belper was never frightened to come and sit down. That was when we was living up West Leake Lane.'

'Now then. The first time we was voting after the war, me mother or father put this poster in the window for vote Labour, and Mr Lewis from the farm [Kingston Fields] he didn't like it because it was vote Labour. Everybody else had got blue. And me mother used to go down to Lewis's to clean.... do their scrubbing and certain other jobs, and she used to do two days up at the Hall. Mr Lewis came in, and he told my mother off in no uncertain terms, that she shouldn't have had that paper in that window. And my mother turned round and told him straight, that she was good enough to clean Lady Belper's floors, and his floors, so why couldn't she have in her window what she chose to put in the window? So Lady Belper happened to be standing in the background, unbeknown to my mother or to Mr Lewis, and she said, "Good for you Mrs Hogg, good for you. I like honesty. You can vote for who you like."'

(Dora Higgins nee Hogg)

Carol & John Taylor in Lady Belper's clothes, Firs Farm, c1950

'**Lady** Belper did come occasionally to [Firs] farm to visit us. I think she came to see my grandmother. Then she used to come and see my mother and very kindly used to pass some clothes on to my mum. Very nice evening clothes, which weren't a great deal of use to my mum, she never went out anyway in the evenings. When I was born - my mum always told me - she [Lady Belper] offered her name, that I should be called by her name which was Angela Mariotta. But my mum declined. She very kindly allowed us to actually go round Kingston Hall grounds, gave us permission to go any time pretty much as we liked, and that was lovely because it was very beautifully laid out. There was a summerhouse, little dogs' cemetery with a summerhouse, there was a boat-house and a couple of bridges, one very big bridge. People would be fishing in the lake; I remember seeing someone once catch a pike. Huge thing!
It was very kind of her actually, we always felt.'

(Carole Easom nee Taylor)

Lady Angela with her sons Peter and Rupert

'**Kingston** Hall staff? Oh yes, there were quite a lot. I'll talk about the ones I know just to give you an inkling, because it was a very large house. We had a butler and two footmen. Then we had a head house maid, did all the cleaning and looking after the bedrooms and so on, and she had two girls under her. Then we had the butler, Mr Allen, and there was a cook Mrs Dawson. Two assistants there, scullery maids I think they were called and so on. So there were about three departments; the butlers department; the house maids department; and the cooking department - so that was nine people.

We also had a considerable number of gardeners under Mr Rowe who was a very expert gardener. I also remember there was a very nice man, but who was always rather coal black. He was called Billy Hardy, he actually lived in Kegworth, and he used to carry the coal. In those days before there was any oil or electric heating it was all done mostly with coal, because there was a lot of coal in that district reasonably cheap. Billy Hardy used to cart the coal about and he always had a black face and black hands - he was quite a character too. So when you consider the gardens - also of course there was the farm - they employed a lot of people.'

'I was very keen on horse riding because my older brother Ronald who was fourth Lord Belper, was a very keen horseman. In fact, he rode in the Grand National twice on a horse called Prime Prince. One year he was fourth, and the next one fifth. Prime Prince was a very good jumper and that's what one needed. But he wasn't a very fast horse, so I don't think there was ever much hope of him winning unless everyone else fell down! But that was quite good for an amateur rider. And my sister Lavinia was very, very keen on riding, and she did a lot to help me. She was a very good rider too, and she used to find suitable ponies for me, because my mother and father weren't quite so well versed in those things. So Lavinia looked after that, and I had some lovely ponies that she got for me. I used to go to gymkhanas and shows and out hunting on these ponies. It was a lovely time.

And we had a groom called Tom Skinner, and he lived in the stables. He was a typical sort .. looked like a little jockey - he was rather keen on the drink though. I remember when we went out riding I wanted to go in nice open fields and have a good canter or gallop, but Tom said "I've got some business to do in Kegworth", and I didn't really realise at that stage what the business was to go to the pub. There was a small pub on the outskirts of Kegworth where he used to go. So he'd get off his horse and ask me to get off, and I would stand there holding his horse and my pony while Tom went away for about twenty minutes and had his beer. But I didn't mind, I was quite happy. One was very laid back in those days. I don't think it was taken very seriously by anybody. But he was quite a character, very much one – or so he told me – for the women, or two.'

(Hon.Peter Strutt)

'When we first moved there in 1924 we lived over the stables. My mother, Charlotte Brownlow, wasn't employed…but she used to help when Miss Lizzie Roberts [head housemaid] wanted help with the house parties. Mum had been in what I'd call 'good gentleman's service'… Miss Roberts was one of the old school, and mum fitted in well and used to help with the housemaids. I can remember going with mum. I'd be in the still room and helped fill some of the jugs – they used to have these copper jugs and washbowls.

Well they used to do a lot of entertaining, Lord & Lady Belper, in the wintertime, we had the shooting parties. I remember once the Duke and Duchess of Portland were there and she had to bring her own maids. There was a lot of fuss about her, 'cos she was one that nobody saw her without her make-up!'

'Lavinia and Michael Strutt, they were very friendly and used to come and play. Her and Michael and Jean Allen, and I think Norah Millburn …one year they had a sledge and they started up by the front door and went zooming right down to the terrace.'

(Muriel Allen nee Brownlow)

Jean Allen & Muriel Brownlow, Kingston, 1928.

'My father Angus MacRae worked on the Estate. He was a forester along with Jack Bent and Bill Stone. They used to maintain a lot of fencing and the woodlands. Latterly, as the number of staff decreased, he worked in the gardens. He carried on working until he was seventy-one years of age.

He originated from Scotland. He was a gillie, and used to go fishing and shooting with the Belper family in Scotland. My mother worked for the Belper family also and used to go up there with Lady Belper, and that's how my parents met, in Scotland.'

' At Christmas time the staff used to have a get-together and have a meal in the staff dining room. I recall my uncle, who was George Laver the butler at the Hall at the time, used to carve the turkey. Then there were usually Christmas presents under the tree for each family.

My aunt Peggy Laver - married to George the butler - was a housemaid. She worked for the Belper family for an awful long time, probably forty years or more. She eventually decided to move back to Scotland in 1979.'

(Ann MacRae)

I understand Lady Belper held Christmas parties at Kingston Hall for the village school children?

'**They** used to come into the Hall, the big area opposite The Terrace, you know. They'd be given a good bun fight and presents. It was all in the evening usually. It was rather sort of romantic, with lights on and all the children, and a lot of laughter going on - excitement for the children. It was quite a big night out for them.'

(Hon.Peter Strutt)

'**I attended** them every year. And Lady Belper bought us all lovely presents, mainly books and jigsaws. Dolls sometimes, depending on the age of the child. I used to think what a lovely place it was and I'd like to work there one day. Years later I did work there and my friend was the housekeeper. '

(Sylvia Church nee Joyce)

'**I only** went to one party. I remember they had a guessing competition – how many peas in a jar. I guessed right and she [Lady Belper] gave me a silver-coloured propelling pencil.'

(George Smith)

(Left) Staff Christmas party. 1948
From left: Peggy Laver, Idelma Chiasserini, ? , Iris.., Lucie.., Lizzie Roberts, Tom Skinner, George Laver (butler), Eliza Curd, Fay Sorrel, Lily Ford (cook), Thomas Waters (footman), Gino Chiasserini.

'**My** grandfather Jack Brown, was head chauffeur for many years. They used to go up to Scotland and things like that. Then when there was not so much driving to do, I think he did a lot of carpentry as well. He had a workshop in the grounds at Kingston Hall.

One thing he did. He used to get up every morning at half past six to put his radio on just to see if the central heating had clicked in up at Kingston Hall, because it used to make a noise. It obviously picked up interference, and if that switched on he was happy. If it didn't he was over there then to make sure it was alright.'

(Jennifer Hutchinson nee Brown)

Master Rupert Strutt, with groom Tommy Skinner, in the back park, Kingston, c1933.

'I had to hire a car when I came for the interview [to work for Ronald, 4th Lord Belper], because there was no direct route from Northampton. First of all, I was interviewed by one of the agents, John German, in the staff sitting room. And when he'd decided that I wasn't such a bad thing, they let me go through to see his Lordship. He was in the study and he sat on this very tall fender, and asked me why I wanted to work for him. I said, well you know I was happy to come as a domestic, and I had been a nanny, but I said I'd never been a cook. He asked me if I could fry eggs and bacon and cook roast beef and Yorkshire pudding. I said, "Yes," he said, "Well you can cook, you can start in May." And that was the end of that. That was May 5th 1971.'

What were your first impressions when you came?

'Well Kingston Hall, it was a very beautiful place. I mean when I had the interview, all I got was sort of the backstairs, into the back way and the staff room. Then, in through a green baize door and into the study - which was off the Terrace Hall - which was a truly impressive, dignified place. Then into the study where his Lordship was, and then back into the kitchen for coffee.

But once I moved here, ah, it was truly impressive, truly impressive. I mean some of the rooms. The library alone, I could have lost myself in there for a week and nobody would have known I was there. Truly beautiful. To see it now is heartbreaking because they've just literally sort of breeze-blocked it up into little units. Well not totally, but compared to what they were, they are you know. To tell you the size of my kitchen - to go from the cooker to the sink is thirty three steps and then back down to the hot cupboard was forty five. And round to the big fridge, which was a long sort of room with a bar at the end where all the vegetables used to be kept - there was this huge catering fridge around the corner, and it was fifty six steps to get from the fridge down to the hot cupboard.'

' When I first started it was my job to cook all the meals, including the staff ones. There was only Joyce and I – she was a young maid from St Helena on a three year exchange – and Peggy, a lovely Scots lady, and her family. She was married to the butler George Laver, and used to work for Lady Herbert of West Leake. We used to call Peggy, Aunty Peggy. You only ever called George, George though!

His Lordship was completely dependent on people looking after him, as was the old aristocracy. Its different now.'

Can you tell us about the other Estate employees at this time?

'Mr Rowe, the head gardener, was a character. He was lovely. He used to come up every morning at half past seven, and on the corner of the kitchen table he would leave me examples of what was ready in the garden. Like if there was peas, if there was beans, a punnet of strawberries, all draped out in leaves and things. All dressed beautifully. Then he would go away and have his breakfast, and I would come down to cook his Lordship's breakfast, and make my list and leave it on the corner of the table. If we wanted plants and things like that we'd put those on the list as well, and he would take the list away. Then one of the boys from the garden would bring a flat cart with all the stuff on, and it was his job to put it away. He was the garden boy, quite a sweet little chap. Then the flowers - we always did the flowers on a Friday - and literally two flat carts of flowers and plants because it was a big Hall.

If we were having guests or a dinner party and the library was going to be open, then we needed three times as many plants.'

'His Lordship's dinner parties, he always liked them to be just so. Even if there was four or forty four. He expected all the silver to be out, and the candelabras. If it was just a small dinner party, say for four, they used the study as the sitting room. But if there was more than four, then you had to open the library out.

If it was a big affair, it entailed an awful lot more work, because not only did you have to do all the flowers, but there was all the silver to bring out of the silver cupboards. The big silver candelabra and the trophies, that obviously for security sake had to be locked away. In those days lots of people still smoked, so silver ashtrays used to have to come out and of course everything had to be cleaned before it was put out. Even though it had been cleaned before it was put away, it still had to be done again. Of course all the candlesticks had to be dressed with special candles and things like this. So before you could do any cooking, you literally had to open the library. And it was just too much for Aunty Peggy to do on her own because she was getting on. She was in her sixties when I went. And so cook came out of the kitchen, and went and interfered in the library, is the long and the short of it.

Then I used to help Joyce with the flowers. His Lordship had a Van Dyke painting in a special place in the library. As you came in, that was what you saw. It was all lit up. We always used to put a special flower display under the Van Dyke in one of the silver cups he'd won at horse racing. When everything was ready house-wise, everybody used to come and help me in the kitchen. So we had a very close family going on in there. But if it was a very big party, then the first years I was there, Alan

Church's wife Sylvia, she used to come over and give a hand, and Shirley Temple, Ron Temple's wife, used to come down. If we needed anybody extra there were several ladies in the village that you knew would come up. But you know, it was lovely to see everything set out looking so splendid, especially with all the big log fires going, and you know, twinkling on the silver and things like that. His Lordship expected a certain standard shall we say.'

' Then there were several other gardeners and part time ladies used to come in. Kath Kirk, she worked on the estate. Her husband Tom, he worked at the farm, and there was two gardeners that lived down in the farmhouses. Then there was Fred Cheshire, the chauffeur; the odd job man and woodman, Harry Woolley; a chap called Alistair; and Angus MacRae, who was Peggy's brother. Then of course the farm workers and gamekeepers.'

'Hunting days we used to have the breakfast first, and then his Lordship used to dress in his hunting kit. But not his red coat; that used to go in the car with his whip and top hat and so forth. He was with the Belvoir Hunt, so they met that way you know, like Eastwell and Cropwell Bishop. He was Master of the Belvoir Hunt, Master of the Quorn Hunt, when I came. I didn't have much to do with it then, because we still had George who did that sort of thing. Then...I seemed to inherit it all. Basically, because Joyce, who was younger than me, was allergic to the horses. She couldn't go anywhere near. She wasn't so bad when the hunting kit was clean; but when it was dirty and smelling of horses, she had to disappear.'

The Greek Temple, Kingston Hall grounds.

'The Greek Temple, that was very beautiful. We used to go there, with Mr Rowe's permission, and read on the steps. Beautiful statues, all on plinths at the top, and these very gracious steps in like York stone – and balustrades coming down – very wide.

I always said, that if ever there'd been a wedding at the Hall, that would have been a wonderful place for the bride to have her photographs taken. But of course when the Hall was sold, the Temple was broken up and sold.'

(Ann Millard)

Hunt Meet at Kingston Hall – 1930s

Work on the Lodge Gates - 1906

Lady Belper's School

'best days of yer life' ?

The school, erected in 1848 by Edward Strutt, MP (created Baron Belper in 1856), was originally a National School. It was extended in 1891 in memory of Emily, 1st Lady Belper. Angela, 3rd Lady Belper, took an active interest in the school and was a great benefactor to it. The school closed on 20 December 1966.

Lady Belper's School, Kingston, 1914.

'When I started school in 1924 they used to divide [partition] it into two…but then [other times] it would be all open. We had assembly, a hymn, and we used to have to learn pieces out of the Bible, the catechism.'

'There was Mrs Dobson, and there was Hilda Daykin – Hilda was a pupil teacher. And then there was Miss Evans, the one that was there a long while.'

'When we were doing knitting…we used to have to knit on four pins and turn a heel on a [sock] thing. I was never very good, but I was worse on gloves. And you had to do that before you could get to do a baby's jacket or something like that. I never got that far!'

'I didn't like Maths much…was never very good at Maths. I liked English, and Drawing, History, Geography and anything like that. Well, we used to do Drill outside… we had no uniform or anything.'

'I vaguely remember us having cocoa to drink…they used to bring it in a jug and we used to have to wash it up in a bowl. I think we had to pay a half-penny for it.'

This was before school milk?

'Oh yes. I'd left before they got school milk.'

What did you do for your meals?

'They used to have to sit in the classroom and have their meal, a sandwich. They came from West Leake you see, and [those] people that came…had to have their meals in the school. There was no school meals as such then.'

(Muriel Allen nee Brownlow)

'**I went** [to Kingston School] from 1928, till I left when I was fourteen. That would be about 1936 when I left school.'

'The teacher when I first went was Miss Stafford. I think she married Alf Moore from Ratcliffe. Then Mrs Foster was Head teacher, and Kitty Evans she was there …and they had a girl that was at school and then went as a junior teacher. Freda Coxon was her name.'

'I remember playing slides because we used to wear - our family coming from Cumberland, Lancashire - what you call 'calkers'. They were irons, on our…clogs. You know what I mean? We wore clogs! And when it was frosty we used to make a slide. Of course I used to make it slippy with using these (clogs) - sliding down the field to go first to make it slippery for the others.'

'We used to jump. Jump the desks! Used to have the desks in the yard for summer you know. They were like them long ones with a seat on them, and we used to try and jump 'em. We did some daredevil things! I used to get the cane occasionally for being late…'cause we had so many jobs to do before we went to school in them days.'

(Ethel Cook nee Marshall)

'**I didn't** like the School Mistress, Mrs Foster. Because as you got older in the class you had to do the boiler…stoke the old boiler up - it were a coal-fired boiler then. I mean, she was one of these teachers that used to hit you for nothing as the saying is. They'd have a fit today if you hit them today like she used to hit you. Any road, I can't remember what I'd done, but she gave me a good clobbering you know. I think I'd perhaps flicked some piece of blotting paper on the ruler across at somebody else, something like that. Any road, I got the stick. So this particular day I'd had enough of the stick, I'd had it that many times. So when I made the boiler up at break time in the middle of the morning, I threw the stick in the boiler and burnt it. Then later on in the morning somebody else had done something wrong, and there she were looking for the stick, wondering where it had gone. So anyway, they ended up having the ruler. So she asked somebody if they could get her a stick, and Margery Vickers says, "I'll bring you one Miss." And she brought this old umbrella shaft you know. Then she did something wrong, and I think she got a dose of that. And it had got the wire on the stick, so I put that in the boiler the next day, out the road.'

(Ron Temple)

'**She** [Lady Belper] used to come and talk to us all and ask how we were doing…with our exams and stuff. We sometimes had to sing things you know, we had to sing for her.'

'She wanted me to go to her school and be a teacher …she used to pay for a tutor for me …you had to go to University in Nottingham, it's the one on Shakespeare Street, three times in the week - the other two you went to Kingston School and looked after the children. Then my mother was taken ill and I didn't go back to the school. I decided [in 1947] to go into the RAF.'

(Sylvia Church nee Joyce)

'**It** would be 1938, I started. I remember when I first went I felt so unhappy being away from home that the teacher used to sit me on the desk, and I used to cry every morning. But she was very nice, she was a lovely teacher. Her name was Kitty Evans…of course I soon settled in after that. I remember I used to dread it when the dentist came and we all had to wait our turn to go in, and be inspected in Mrs Yardley's house. Well that was awful. And I remember the nit nurse coming.'

'Mrs Foster, she was Head Teacher. She was very strict, but she was very good. I remember that she used to be reading to us, and she used to sit on the front bench facing us all. Unfortunately her dress didn't cover everything, and we could see all her bloomers with the elastic round the bottom coming down to her knees! The last years I was there, more or less the last 12 months, I used to get Kitty Evan's bike, and Mrs Foster used to send me up to her own home in Kegworth to collect the mail.'

(Christine Whitehead nee Joyce)

'**I was** in short trousers at the time, which I think had a couple of patches - on the backside of me trousers which I used to go to school in. I also used to wear a pair of Dutch clogs with the old iron rim on the bottom. You could hear me clopping up the road when I was on me way to school in the morning, and coming back at night. On the way to school, just as you went over Kingston Bridge out of the village towards the school, there were three beech trees on the right hand side. And we used to collect a handful or so of beechnuts off the path as we went down, to sort of break open and eat later at school.'

'My first teacher was Miss Evans. She came from Normanton-on-Soar. As you went up in form the next teacher was Miss Foster; she was the head teacher. Everybody has their miss days, and I did actually feel the cane one or two times across the end of me fingers off Miss Foster. She was definitely a crack shot with a cane she was, across the ends of yer fingers!'

'They were basic the lessons, Reading, Writing and your Maths or sums, whatever we used to call them in them days. But I think we did learn quite a lot.'

'Then…me and quite a few more of the children from the village …we went on from Kingston to Gotham to finish our schooling days. We left at 15.'

(George Vickers)

'**My** first memory was going [from Kingston Fields] across Kingston Park to school by the pond, which I don't think is there anymore. That's been filled in. Then we met up with Christine and Sylvia Joyce and there was Vera Kitchen and Leonard Kitchen. But yes, going across the irons [cattle grid] at Kingston, so far across the park…and seeing in the distance Pat, and Doug, and Peter Hill coming from the farm that's near the Kingston Hall gardens. Then we all cut through the Hall grounds to get to the top of the hill. You could actually go through the Coal Road Gate, which I suppose we should have done really, but we didn't do that. We used to take us life in us hands going through the Hall grounds, because they had some little dogs that used to chase runners. I think they belonged to Ronald Strutt at the time, and they was looked after by…the butler, George Laver. A little grey dog – it used to run after you if it happened to be out. Oh dear!'

'We used to have to take sandwiches to school, and towards lunch-time Mrs Foster used to come in and give Miss Evans the eggs to go on the boil on this big round stove they had in the little classroom. Each child more or less had a turn in doing this, but there were certain ones that used to forget they'd got to do it. They would go off playing and forget they'd to put those eggs on. And then one day I was asked to do it, and I actually remembered to do it…that's about the only thing at that school that I did get right.!'

Can you remember the games you played?

'One day in particular - in the summertime we used to do lessons in the yard on the old fashioned desks and then we had games in the park, just over the fencing - and this day we bent down and the others were jumping over us backs; I can't remember what it was called now. Anyway these boys were jumping over us backs and all going round. We was having a lovely time. Next thing Miss Evans came out, blew the whistle, and we had to go in. They had been standing at the window looking out the window, and what we hadn't appreciated was - I'll not name names - but some of these here boys when we was bending down they was trying to see how far up our legs they could see. So that was a good game! Then there was another day when we were playing rounders…and of course we got going round and round, and then it came to my turn to hit the ball. Slam! And I ran, got round, and the next person that did it they threw their bat and hit me straight across my nose. So I had a sizeable nose bleed.'

'And of course we used to go at least once a week on a nature walk. We used to walk all across the park and go all round the Lake. Cut through certain parts…where you go over the little bridges, and all the way round. And then back down the other side of the Lake, and back down to school - a whole afternoon. Then the next day we were supposed to write down what we've experienced on that walk. We used to love that.'

'Eventually… we had canteen dinners that was prepared by Miss Webster and a Mrs Henson, and Mrs Henderson used to help at the school canteen. When it first began there, we used to have it in a large room at the Village Hall, and then it finished up us having it in the smaller room at the back. We used to have some beautiful meals in that canteen.
One day in a week we always had a cheese dish. And we always knew that when we had this cheese dish it would be followed by a chocolate pudding and a chocolate sauce. Of course we could have seconds, and sometimes we had thirds. Marvelous!
We always had a cup, or a glass of water on the table. Of course there used to be two girls out the main class – standard - they used to go down at a certain time in the morning to help lay the tables and put the water out.'

'The very first Christmas Nativity play I can remember, when we first went to live at Kingston [in 1940], the children performed on the stage [at the Village Hall] with a screen in front of them so all you could see was the shadows. It was very nicely done, and I've never ever known it to be done since. There was people talking, and it was behind this screen. You couldn't see who was doing that part, but that was very nice, and very unusual.'

'At least once a year we used to have to put our own show on - we all had to do something on the stage, and Lady Belper used to come and sit, and of course the school teacher. I can never ever re-member the parents coming; but the whole class used to sit there, and we all had something to do. Vera Kitchen, Sylvia Joyce, myself and Christine Joyce we used to have to do a dance because the vicar's wife - Mr New's wife - had taught us to do this dance [in order] to do something at a garden party they'd held at West Leake Manor. I just can't remember the year we did that, but it wasn't long after that Mr New went in the army. We used to do this here particular dance on stage, us four…. It was tap tap here, and then up and out, and tap tap there and up and out again!'

(Dora Higgins nee Hogg)

'**I used** to come [to school] by bus from West Leake. We moved here [Kingston] in May 1950. We came to the Village Hall for our school dinners in the Coronation Room – two of my pet hates were swedes and turnip. I also used to hate figs – sometimes we'd get figs as a pudding. I don't recall getting the cane, no. Or the rubber thrown at me!'

In the primary school with Miss Evans it was a solid fuel fire they had. Mr Yardley …one of the school caretakers, I remember him having to come in with a shovel of coal and keep the fire stoked up. I think they were quite happy days really at Kingston School.'

(Ann MaCrae)

Carole Taylor at school, c1954

'**I remember** my first day there…in 1950, going into the big classroom and the sun shining through the windows. I went on the back of mum's bike [from Firs Farm] – I had a little seat on the back..'

'I remember the country dancing because I got smacked on the legs once by Miss Evans – 'twanked' on the legs, as she used to call it.'

'I remember Nature Walks more than anything, walking up and around Kingston Hall, around the grounds. We used to sit under the trees drawing things – leaves and that type of thing.'

Do you remember Lady Belper visiting the school?

'She always seemed very kind. She used to bring us a lot of gifts at school. Different things like cocoa powder, and sweets as well at one time. I can remember her presenting a Coronation mug and a New Testament'

Outdoor lesson in Kingston Park, 1951
From left: Frank Reynolds, Jennifer Brown, Joan Madeley, …. , …. ,…. ,…. , Jean Brown, Ann Knight, ….. Standing: Enda Hogg and Tony Smith . Headmaster is Oliver B.Smith.

The School Log Book entry for 22 April 1953 reads : Children invited by Lady Belper to Kingston Hall to see her Coronation Robes.

'I can remember seeing them…remember them being draped, and also the little coronets they wore.'

(Jennifer Hutchinson nee Brown)

'We had radio broadcasts…programmes on the radio for lessons at times – a big radio, a huge thing in the classroom….In the summer on one or two occasions [we went] into the park and sat and did our sewing with Mrs Surridge [needlework teacher].

(Carole Easom nee Taylor)

'**I started** just after Christmas, early 1950. I used to walk to Kingston from the Lodge [on West Leake Lane]. Mr Smith was the head teacher in the junior side …superseded by Mr Williams who lived locally.'

'Did I get the cane? No. I was lucky I think. I can remember one particular incident …we used to able to play in the park outside the school, it was snowing this particular day, and of course you know what lads are like with snowballs. We were throwing them at a lorry going past and unfortunately he'd got his window open, and he wasn't amused. It went in and he come back and told the teachers about it, and we got hauled over the coals for that! But we didn't actually get the cane.'

I understand you were in the football team?

'Oh yeah, notorious that. I'd rather not think about that to be honest; I was the goalkeeper! The only match I remember playing was at Sutton Bonington – against Sutton School – and we lost about 6-nil, I think…it was partly down to me.'

(Leslie Joyce)

'**I was** head girl of Kingston School. I used to take the dinner numbers down to the two ladies who used to prepare the meals. At this time there was a footbridge built at the side of the bridge over the brook, to take pedestrians because…traffic was increasing somewhat. I do remember the whole of the school standing on this bridge with Mr Williams and Miss Evans – I know there were photographs taken.'

'We did an awful lot of craftwork. I can't remember doing such a lot of academic work but we certainly must have done, because I did a calculation once of how many of my peer group went on to pass some sort of examination or another, and I think it was between 70 and 80%. So we certainly must have had a very good grounding.'

'We used to do…raffia mats, dolls clothes, needlework and canework : and have sales of work. Quite a big event.'

Lady Belper's School Football Team, 1956
Back Row: Paul Winson, Raymond North, Richard Doyle, Leslie Joyce , Alan Tongue, John Fowell
Front Row: Chris Bracey, Bob James, Ian MacRae, Leslie Knight, Richard Harrison.
Headmaster, Mr Williams

'We did a lot of singing, all the lovely old songs, folk songs I suppose they were – 'Hearts of Oak' and 'Over the Sea to Skye'. Lots of Country Dancing, the Cumberland Reel comes to mind. I loved country dancing.'

'I remember the school was divided into the little room and the big room, and Miss Evans was the teacher of the infants. I think we were about seven when we went up into the big room. First of all Mr Smith was the Head master, then Mr.Williams. Miss Evans – who we used to call 'Kitty Blue-Eyes'- she actually taught my mum [Bertha Higgins] and my aunts and uncles a generation before, as well as teaching me and my brothers. She told me one thing that I've remembered until now - I must have been only six-ish. And that was, that when you get up in the morning you are supposed to blow your nose very, very loud and very long, and it clears the sinuses out for the day. And that's the secret of a very healthy and long life!'

Handicraft Lesson, 1951
From Left: Joan Madeley, Margaret Newsome, Jean Brown, ……

'We used to have third of a pint milk bottles, with cardboard tops, and with these tops we used to make pom-poms – wind wool round, and make pom-poms on them.

We used to have seasons for playing games like whip and top. That used to be at Easter time; and we used to play conkers, obviously in the Autumn; and we had a season for marbles. We used to do roller-skating…play dice…and have a skipping season, skipping independently, but also with the huge skipping ropes that we used from school. They were really great big things, and they had a turner on each end. We probably had ten or twelve children skipping in this rope.'

"All in together girls" – Skipping at school, 1951
(From left: Thelma North, Brenda Madeley, Carole Taylor, Dolly Vickers, Wendy North, Anthea Daykin)

'Christmas was quite a special time at school. We used to have a biggish Nativity Play in the Village Hall…the last two or three years I sang and I used to get to play Mary which was the star.

Sometimes, Lady Belper used to come down and present us with one or two little things. If my memory serves me right, we were given a quarter pound of Dairy Box chocolates…something completely different for us, and a huge Jaffa orange. And I suppose after the war – this wasn't too long after the war – you couldn't get a lot of fresh fruit and things like that. So that was always very special.'

(Maureen May nee Winson)

' **I remember** the school very vividly, not enjoying myself there very much. I found it very hard, not a very good scholar unfortunately. I was very, very poor at spelling. I was put on a lot with the teachers there, and in them days they used to sit over you or stand over you while you did it. And reading as well, wasn't very easy. It was Mr Williams more so than Miss Evans, that was very strict…very strict.'

' Summer days, we'd walk to school, or go on the bikes, because mum couldn't afford to pay for the bus fare. But in the winter we always went on the bus, on the South Notts bus. It used to go all round West Leake, Lantern Lane, then down into Ratcliffe, and back to Kingston School.'

And did you stay for the school dinners?

'Yes, we used to walk from Kingston School down into Kingston Village Hall, and I also remember there having dinner one day and I've never ate it since, I was stood over and made to eat bread and butter pudding, and I've never touched it in my life ever since. Miss Evans, "Now you will eat it. You will!" You know, it was awful. Most of the dinners weren't very good. I think they used to come from County Hall, Nottingham, somewhere. They used to bring them in big aluminium containers.'

'I can remember precisely, towards the end of maybe a Christmas term, when you all used to have what they'd call today an activity day, you know, where there's no lessons. We all stood round the piano in Miss Evans' class - I'd only be about seven - and Miss Evans was asking what everybody wanted to do when they left school. All the girls were talking, you know, different things. And I can remember exactly to this day, Miss Evans asking me what I'd like to do. And I said, "Well one day I'm going to have a Bus Company." And everybody laughed, I always remember that - but there you are, it's come true!'

(Paul Winson)

'**I attended** the school 1964-66 [up to its closure]. Mr Williams and Mrs Reeves were rather strict. When we sat down for our school dinners at the Village Hall we had to place our hands on the table for them to be inspected, both sides, to make sure they were clean. They also ensured we were sitting straight upright, with our shoulders pressed against the back of the chair. I recall nature films with a projector, also radio programmes. We once had an art competition, and I drew a picture of Lord Belper in a yellow suit, walking in the Hall grounds, for which I won a prize – a book of poems.'

(Sue Woolley nee Nolan)

Final year at Kingston School – 1966

Left: Headmaster J.L.Williams. Right: Teacher Mrs E.Reeves

Front Row: Gary Boden (kneeling), Paul Melkis, Adrian Hannah, Danny Anderson, - , Russell Case, John Dennet, Christopher Potts, David Stone, Marius…
2nd Row: Andrew Perkins (standing), Sue Nolan, Rosie Cousins, - , Sheila North, Anna Temple, Denise Roper, Lorna Potts, - , Heather Cousins, - , David Perkins.
3rd Row: Daniel Anderson, Paul Temple, Norma Bertram, John Stone, Keith Courtman, Adrian Eaves, Judy Melkis, Andrew Watnall, Barbara Hannah.
Back Row: Kevin Jones, Alan Boden, - , Janette Dennet, Richard North, Andrew Humphrey, Geoff Stone.

Lady Belper's School – 1928

Front Row(L to R): Bertha Higgins, Muriel Vickers, Vera Marshall, Sheila Jones, Bill Maltby, Ruth Vickers, Jack Hall, Wilfred Higgins, Mabel Elliot, Roy Hall.

Second Row: Tom Buckley, Ken Easom, Ken Kerry, Elsie Poxon, Grace Hall, Sheila Elliott, Gwen Jones, Joan Beswick, Hilda Powell, Ethel Marshall, Pam McCartney, Douglas Easom.

Third Row: Jessie Elliott, Margaret Harris, Mabel Yates, Ada Brittan, Joyce Vickers, Mary Smith, Hilda Green, Lilian Easom, Lilian Kent, Ivy Kerry, May Dewsbury, John Chadburn.

Fourth Row: Renee Milburn, Arthur Kerry, Robert Kent, Ron Taylor, Arthur Easom, Michael Jones, Norman Elliott, Terence Jones, Ernest Higgins, Walter Powell, Freda Coxon.

Back Row: Tom Kirk, Jack Higgins, Arthur Powell, Dennis Jones, George Maltby, John Spencer, Les Powell, Mick Easom.

Kingston Gypsum Mine

'one tub up at a time'

The Kingston Gypsum Company was formed by Henry, 2nd Lord Belper, in 1880. Managed by the Woodfield family for most of its life, it was a major employer in the area for over a hundred years. The mine closed in the early 1980s, and the Works were demolished in 1986. The site is now occupied by a haulage firm, T. Baden Hardstaff Ltd.

Kingston Gypsum Mine, 1956

'My grandfather was asked by Baron Belper the Second, to sink a shaft on the Kingston Estate in 1880, I believe, and that he did. A few years later a railway line was laid down to the wharf at Kingston-on-Soar, and the gypsum was transported down the railway line to the wharf in a truck drawn by horses. The gypsum was loaded into barges at the wharf at Kingston, and moved on to Barrow-on-Soar where it was ground into powder. In 1888 the first mill building was built at Kingston. It was supplied by a firm in Newark-on-Trent called Wakes and Lamb, and it consisted of about eight pairs of millstones - French burr stones and Derbyshire grey stones - and they ground the gypsum into fine powder. The gypsum, as I said, was transported down to the wharf and drawn by horses. Well, we had so many fatalities with the horses, that an old steam loco was bought to replace them, and it was called Lady Margaret after Lady Belper. Another loco was bought in 1926 that was brand new. It came from Pecketts of Bristol, and was named Lady Angela, after the next Lady Belper. That locomotive, when we finished with it - I got a replacement in a diesel because it was far more economical to use - was transferred to various places, but ended up at Buckfastleigh in Devon and was completely rebuilt and repainted in it's original livery. I believe she's still working today on the privately owned steam engine railway track down there.'

'In the early days we had pit ponies. The men used to drill the face of gypsum with hand augers which had to be kept sharpened and tempered by a blacksmith that we had on the works site. They drilled the holes then charged them with, I believe gelignite, or gelignol, and fired. Then all the blown gypsum was hand loaded into wooden tubs and drawn by the ponies to the pit bottom. The tubs were loaded into a cage, one at a time, and taken up to the surface. One tub up at a time.'

'Above the main seam of gypsum there was one fairly thick seam, about two or three feet, which was very high quality and it was called Ball Stones. It was often in the shape of balls. That used to be mined quite separately - a rather treacherous task - on trestles. And it was kept separate from the rest of the gypsum. That came out and went to a seperate section on the surface to be hand cleaned for very high quality purposes. All the marl and impurities were chopped off with a hand chopper. We later used little compressed air hammers with a chisel in the end, and they [the men] used to go round each lump of gypsum and clean off all the marl and impurities. If there was a vein that went through it, they had to split the lump of gypsum down the vein and then clean both faces of that vein. That produced a very high quality gypsum - 99% plus. And in order to outdo our neighbours, who used to do the same sort of thing, we used to add Reckitt's Blue, mix it with water, and spray all these lumps of gypsum before it was further processed - ground and processed - to make it whiter than white.'

'The men were often paid on the weight and quality, and they had a habit of putting some rather low quality gypsum in the bottom of the tub, and then putting all the good high quality stuff on the top. When this was found out - because each tub was tipped into a big primary presser – a scheme of putting dots against each of the team of men down below [was introduced]. When they got nine dots against their name they were penalised, either by a reduction in their bonus, or a stoppage of their bonus.'

Could you explain how the gypsum rock was processed to make plaster?

After it came out of the mine, it went through a crushing and screening plant, and was loaded - large lumps, about eight inch down to plus three inch - into nine kilns, in which we made a very special type of plaster called Sirapite. The name originated from the name Plaster of Paris. "Sirapite" is Paris written backwards, with 'ite' on the end.'

The Mine and Mill, c1905

'It was used for plastering walls and ceilings of houses, and also round the dados of hospitals and schools. Because it was a rather tough, harder type of plaster than that made by all the other Works. It was also used round the window reveals and door frames, where it would get hard wear and tear. It was a secret process. Each of the Gypsum under-takings in the Country originated by being family or privately owned businesses, that went back to the early 1800s – 1830, or 40. When we were taken over by British Plaster Board in the mid-1930s, although we were a big company, we still competed against one another. And what each Works did, that was very private and secret to anybody else. Well this process of ours, in these high-powered kilns, was very specialised, and the men were instructed to keep people out, and the doors to be kept shut all the time. Baron Belper the third, who was very close to my father - great friends - he used to take a lot of interest in the Kingston Works and came down regularly. There was one occasion when he visited the office, came in and asked to see Woodfield, and he was duly asked to take a seat whilst somebody went across into the Works to fetch him. Lord Belper wouldn't hear of that, he said "No, I'll go and find him myself." So he walked across into the Works, opened the door of this department, which was supposed to be all hush-hush, and one of the operatives saw him walk in and went up to him and said, "I'm sorry you're not allowed in here. Will you please go?" And Lord Belper said, "Do you know who I am?" He said, "No I don't." "Well," he said "I'm Lord Belper," and the operative said, "Well I don't mind whether you're the King of England. Will you please get out, you're not allowed in here." And Lord Belper did as he was told, and when he did meet up with my father he had to admit that he was very impressed by the loyalty of the men.'

(Richard Woodfield)

Bags of Sirapite, Kingston Mine

'I started at Kingston Mine [in 1929, aged 14] at 15/8d [78p] a week, fifty-four hours, and I did about every job on the firm before I left. I was there about seven years.'

What were the conditions like?

'Terrible. You were just a slave. When you went to collect your pay you were supposed to salute. Some of the chaps were sarcastic about it, but didn't let it show. But I wouldn't. They made me wait till they paid everybody else. I think I was a bit of a rebel all the while I worked there, and I got all the dirty jobs. I can't remember the first job, but eventually I got a job mending bags. I reckon I mended about 2,000 out of 10,000. All the others were rotten. The chap in charge of the bag room kept a record of what I did, how many I had to throw away. I had to cart them down the length of the firm, and burn 'em on the tip. I kept a fire going for weeks.'

' When I finished that job, then I went on bagging stuff off the grinding machines in the bottom of the Mill. Then I gradually got moved all over the place. I got a job sample taking, checking the quality of all the different sorts of plaster and cement they were making, recording it, and the setting time and colour. You see, I was more or less fully trained when I was seventeen and I knew all the processes.'

'Jack [my brother] and me dad [John William] they worked down the pit. They were 'blowing'. Used explosives to blow the stone out, then load it and put it in trucks, and it come up on the cage'.

' I got the job of what they call check weighman. You were more or less out in the open. Freezing weather it were, I remember, in the snow and ice. You had to pull the wagons off the cage, put empty on, then take the full one onto the weighing machine, and weigh it and record it. Well, I got into trouble over that, because I put the proper weight down. They were only allowed 18 cwts. Well a lot of them would have 21 on, so I just kept that on the side - 3 cwts on the side - and put it in if they sent one short. But I weren't allowed to do that, and I got moved. The boss come and checked me up a time or two, and told me to put the proper weights down - that only eighteen were the limit, any other you didn't record. I says, "Well how do you make that out?" "The chaps are not getting paid for that then?". "Oh, that's got nothing to do with you," he used to say …and then he sacked me from that job. I got pushed into the hottest part of the firm then where …. the stuff was in the big kilns, and it were red hot when they drew it out, and my job were to pull it out level on the floor so it would kill quicker. And it used to burn the skin off you nearly. I mean, it were like going from winter to summer in a day. I tell you it were slavery. I mean, I wasn't the only one. They were lads my age shovelling that into barrows, and wheeling it into the big machines, crushers, all day long and they were on the same wage as me.'

Mine workers, c1931 – George Smith in centre

'…and what brought it all to a head was that all the men decided to join the Union at Gotham. Well, they picked me out, I think because nobody else wanted the job, to be on the committee, to go and meet the management periodically. You know how Unions were. But eventually he [the boss] found out not many days after, we had been to this Union meeting. He come down and he said, "You either come out the Union or you lose this job." I said, "Well I've already lost it then haven't I?" Cos' I stuck to the Union and I payed it the rest of my life. I got the sack; well I sacked myself when I was twenty-one, when I could please myself .'

' They stopped me dole, and I had to go to Donington, walk it to Castle Donington. There were no dole, and the manager says, "You can have ten shillings [50p] Poor Relief. And that's what I did. I used to have to go to Nottingham, walk it to Lenton, fetch this ten shillings a week, and I used to give that to me mother to keep me. Odd times I rode back if it were wet or anything like that, but I'd rather walk it than pay the bus fare. It were only sixpence I think, but it were better for me to have that sixpence than the bus company.'

(George Smith)

'**I qualified** as an engineer at Loughborough University, or Loughborough College as it was then, and I was contacted by a member of the Company and asked why I hadn't joined. The long and short of it was that I did eventually join up on September 3rd 1950, which happened to be the very same day that my father had joined as well, September 3rd. I was at Kingston for only fifteen years. My grandfather did forty years, my father did fifty-five years, and I did fifteen at Kingston although I did thirty, nearly forty years with the Company.'

Was the reconstruction after World War II good for the Gypsum business?

'It was indeed, very good. With all the rebuilding work that had to take place after all the bomb damage up and down the country, it's another instance of people benefiting from other people's misfortunes. And of course the whole of our Company was very busy producing building plasters to satisfy the very large scale building programme that was in force at the time.'

I believe the 1953 floods were also beneficial to the Company?

'A lot of the land on the east coast was flooded and I believe the Dutch people had found that grinding Gypsum to a fairly course specification was very good for reclaiming the land and getting it back into agricultural use much quicker. The effect was for the Gypsum to absorb the salts that were left behind by the sea water. So we started to produce this course ground gypsum called for by the Ministry of Agriculture. We worked twenty four hours a day, seven days a week, sending as many thousands of tons as we could to reclaim land on the east coast.'

Could you tell us about the Mine in the post-war period?

'After the hand-gotten days, I think it was towards the end of the 1940s, 1946 or 47, we introduced some scrape-hauler units, which actually scraped up the gypsum that had been blasted from the face and loaded it onto a conveyor belt, which then fed the steel tubs. We had to go from wooden tubs to steel tubs when we got a little more mechanised. We did away with the ponies, and we introduced small Ruston diesel locos down below ground as well, to haul the loaded trucks to the pit bottom.'

'About 1957, I think, the Adit was completed. It was done so that we could even further mechanise the system down below ground. The company had found that tractors and trailers were a very useful mobile unit, as opposed to tracks below ground which had to be rigid. And so we drove this drift, and we started from below to come up to the surface. Work was going rather slowly, and in order to speed the plough, the contractors decided that they would start from up on the surface and go down to meet those coming up from underground. We had some awful worries at one time that we weren't going to meet, but I think we did meet very well, with only three or four inches out.

We did eventually connect up with Gotham Mine. But the adit was nothing to do with Gotham, it was purely for Kingston purposes.'

(Richard Woodfield)

New Steel Headgear, 1947

'A lot of gypsum was crushed down to minus an inch, inch and a half, and many hundreds of tons were despatched each week to the Portland Cement manufacturers. That was always sent off.. Most of it went by rail - Rugby Portland Cement, Chinner Cement Company, Abberthaw, to name but a few. They couldn't make Portland Cement without the use of gypsum in it, and it was added, I believe, to the small extent of 4%, and it was used as an accelerator. That means that the neat Portland Cement wouldn't set, it had no specific setting time at all. But the addition of gypsum brought the set back to what ever they wanted it to be, and it was regulated by the addition of the gypsum.'

'Now, a lot of that white, ultra white, superfine white gypsum went for mainly two purposes from Kingston. One was a brewers gypsum, and we sent quite a bit to the breweries at Burton-on-Trent. That was to harden the water, because you can't make good beer without hard water. The other use was we sent a lot up to a firm called British Arkady in Manchester who made flour [for] bread making - and they used to add this finely ground, superfine gypsum to their process. So we ate it as well! There were some other uses. I mean it can be, and is still used in cosmetics, I believe. It's more of a filler to carry the smaller amounts of perfume and such like. And of course, it's used in dental and surgical plasters.'

(Richard Woodfield)

'**When** I left school, I started work at the Gypsum Mines at Kingston. I was the office junior there initially. I used to work on the switchboard. Mr Jack Robey was our Office Manager, and he was quite strict. As we arrived for work in the morning we used to have to knock on his door and say, "Good morning Mr Robey," and then at the end of the day, before we went home, we had to go and knock on his door and say, "Good night," to him. I was told not to start laughing when I was at work otherwise people would think I hadn't got enough work to do. So I had to be very quiet, and very diligent, just get on with your work and no chatting. I was the only female there working in the office at that time.'

How long did you work there?

'From 1958 to 1971. So that was thirteen years. Initially, I used to cycle to work, but then there was a lorry used to transport people to and from work, so eventually I used to get a lift on the lorry. I had to climb into the back of the lorry – with all the men!'

(Ann MacRae)

'**I was** the chemist and I set up a laboratory at the Gypsum Mine at Kingston for Dick Woodfield [in 1957], mainly for the analysis of the gypsum out of the mine, control of the plasters that were produced, and also to check the air in the mine itself. I was responsible for checking any bad air down in the mine, which I used to go down about once a month, or if necessary, more frequent depending on the situation down there. Later, there was diesel locomotives down there, dirty old things. After that they had tractors hauling the rock out, and we used to have to check the exhaust from the tractors.'

' It was reasonably good down there, mainly because of the amount of air space. Of course the roof was very high – it was eight or ten feet in places. You could have gone round in a double decker bus!'

Kingston Mine – 1956

'In the 1950s when I started conditions were reasonably good but it was old-fashioned. There wasn't any development and very little alteration the whole of the time I was there. The methods of manufacture; a lot of it was what they call pan plaster, which was an early, very old, method of calcining gypsum; and they also had bottle kilns where the anhydrous plaster [Sirapite] was produced. How many employees? 150, I should say roughly – a lot down the mine.'

These houses in Kingston where I live now were built for British Gypsum. They were built to house some of the employees of Kingston Works, but the opportunity was also taken to use them for experimental plaster work. As far as I am aware there is none of them exactly the same. For instance, the one I live in is plastered. We're the only ones that's actually plastered in the traditional way, but the rest are known as dry lining. It was experimental at that stage, where they put up the panels of plaster board onto wood, and also what they call the egg box type of plaster where there are two plaster boards with cardboard interwoven in between. They tried all these because it was something that they knew they were developing, and these houses were used for that purpose.'

So these houses were some of the first where those products were actually used?

'Yes. Mainly to see how it worked out.'

(Arthur Dale)

Kingston Mine closed in the early 1980s. Can you say why?

'**Well,** it closed after a hundred years. We ran out of reserves mainly. All the gypsum was worked up, and shortly afterwards of course the Gotham Works closed down as well.'

(Richard Woodfield)

Kingston Mine in 1983

Demolition of Works. July 1986

The Gypsum Railway

'you could see sparks flying when it got speed up'

The three mile long railway was constructed in 1883 to connect the Gypsum Mine with the Midland Railway at Kegworth Station. Steam locomotives Lady Margaret (Falcon, 1885) and Lady Angela (Peckett, 1926), and later a Ruston & Hornsby diesel locomotive (1963) worked the line. The railway closed in 1970 when the Company decided to transport all products by road.

Lady Angela crossing Gotham Road towards Kingston Mine, 1962

'**With** living in Kingston I used to know the old gentleman George Daykin, who used to drive the Lady Margaret which was the first train on the Gypsum Line. It run between Kingston Gypsum Mine and Kegworth sidings. Later years, the train was swapped …they changed over to what they called Lady Angela, a similar model to the Lady Margaret. By that time, George Daykin had retired as one of the older train drivers and there was Tommy Hutchinson from Kegworth. He used to drive the Lady Angela. The fireman on it was George Yardley, from out the village. He used to live at the school house, at the old Kingston School. Later, Walter Powell took over as the stoker on the engine, and a bit of time later he was actually driving the trains every so often, when Tommy his driver, was either ill or something like that. He'd gained enough experience to actually take the train over and keep the job going while Tom was on holiday.'

'There have been times when the train come off. The maintenance on the track itself wasn't very great. There were only one chap who used to maintain the track, and I mean, one chap on his own couldn't exactly do it, there's that much work to do. Changing sleepers and jacking the line up, things like that is not what a chap can do on his own. Lets see, the train went down in the morning; he used to come back again at about half 12; go back again about 2 in the afternoon, and then come up again between 5 and 6 at night. He used to bring about 4 trucks each time he come up, 4 trucks of gypsum plaster. The chap who maintained the line, George Yardley, he'd have chance to do so many jobs, but he couldn't keep it up to standard, not on his own.'

'And I think what happened one day there were probably a couple of rotten sleepers in the track and the the line splayed out - the train come off through the rotten sleepers. That were down near the dog kennels, on that stretch.'

(George Vickers)

'**I were** in charge of the loading gang at that time, when I was at the pit, and the engine would push out ten or twelve box cars, as they call them, right up. Went right up to the office. Then we started loading the first one near the engine, then dropped it down as you loaded 'em you know. Well the engine driver had gone…and we wanted this engine to bring down one [wagon]. So I nips into the cab and took the brake off and pushed the throttle open, and of course, not being used to it, it were a bit too hard, and it bellowed out and skidded the wheels you know. And anyway, I stopped it at the right place. But before I could get out, the boss and this engine driver had come and played hell with me.'

'Another time, I don't know what happened actually, but the engine [Lady Angela] got away. It were pouring with rain and the driver hadn't wound the brake on tight enough to hold it, and gradually, when the metals got wet, it started to slip. Of course nobody could catch it, and it went right up to Kegworth through all the gates. How many is there? There's one on West Leake Lane by the houses, one on the road to Kingston, one on the road to Ratcliffe and it loops right round, and then going up towards the Station. It broke through all them gates, it must have been going like an express. It wasn't running at all [in steam], it was just you know, sliding. When they had this inquest into it, it had made flats on the engine wheels with it skidding. You could see sparks flying when it got full speed up!'

(George Smith)

'**The** engines from the mine were called the Lady Margaret her [my mother's] mother-in-law, and also her self Lady Angela. They used to take the gypsum from the mine up to Kegworth Station.

That was another excitement in our life to go along with Mr Daykin the engine driver for a trip on the train from the mine up to the main line.'

Lady Angela shunting at Kingston Mine. August 1955

You used to go on the footplate?

'On the engine, yes! That was very exciting. You can imagine that, because everyone wanted to be an engine driver in those days. It was lovely.'

(Hon. Peter Strutt)

'**The** one train I remember was called Lady Angela. We used to call her 'Angie', and you could set your clock by Angie. When Angie went by I should have been back at school after lunch. I was always late, Angie had gone, and I was racing to school. That was about a field away from the farm [Firs Farm], the railway.'

(Carol Easom nee Taylor)

'**Another** treat when we were riding to and from school, was to actually get to the railway line to see the Lady Angela. We used to just pedal like hell and just get there – you could hear the train – I don't know whether the train drivers used to look out for us. I think they used to just blow the whistle and hope that we got there…it was like 'The Railway Children', very romantic!

I just loved the noise of it rattling by, the metal on metal I suppose. And it used to screech and grunt and complain. We just stopped there and watched it till it was out of sight.'

(Maureen May nee Winson)

'**Lady** Angela. We used to go and meet it at the crossing, just between the cottages on West Leake Lane, and we used to ride on the engine right through to the other side of Kingston village.

If there was a couple of us went up, they would allow us to go on the footplate and just ride with them. And they used to put us off near Beeby's farm and then we would walk back.'

(Paul Winson)

'**I remember** Lady Angela and the gypsum line that came by the village - at the back of the village. Generally when the line was operational I was at school, except in the summer and the other holidays. On occasions when the diesel locomotive that they used was either in for service or repair, or refused to work, they would steam Lady Angela.

Now my ears are tuned to the sound of when Lady Angela was around, and if I happened to be off school I would dash out into the fields to see her go past. I would dash down the village underneath the main railway and go up to the first level-crossing [on Ratcliffe Lane] as she came under. She'd go across the road, and if I was very lucky I would be able to be sneaked aboard on the footplate and have a brief ride round until they got over the brook and round by the field. Then I would have to get off again, before they crossed the road and went on to the embankment where the exchange sidings were, because that was British Rail, and of course the health and safety prevailed there.'

(Stuart Dale)

Lady Angela at Kingston Mine - 1970   (Gerald North on footplate)

RCTS Kingston Gypsum Tour, Kegworth Siding 10th September 1960 (Fireman Sandy Powell in foreground)

Lady Angela leaving Kingston Mine – May 1971

Farming & Agriculture

'yer put a lot of hours in for the money yer got'

In the early 20th century there were three major farms in Kingston – Church, Manor, and Kingston Fields. The latter was occupied by the Midland Dairy College until 1928, and is now farmed by the Estate. Two smaller farms - Oaks Farm and Firs Farm - situated on Gotham Road, ceased operations and the buildings have been converted to two private dwellings.

Steam ploughing on Kingston Fields Farm (Jack Beeby on engine)

'We were married in 1943, and we came to live in Kingston [Church Farm]. We were using horses at the time, although we did have a tractor as well. But we had five lovely horses, and a wagoner to look after them named Bob Shaw.'

Do you remember ploughing and harvesting with horses?

'I do indeed. Very hard work. Hay making was terrible, everything was done with pitchforks and it was very physical, very manual, very hot. We used to have to work very long days. Not only were we hay making, we were milking the cows at the same time, because we had a milking herd.. We went on till ten o'clock at night, and then up at five o'clock in the morning to milk the cows.'

'We were employing five men at that time, with some casual labour as well. When we were growing sugar beet we had a lot of Irish labour to pull the sugar beet. They came over from Ireland. We also used to have women for picking potatoes - there was a lot of manual work.'

What do you recall about your first tractor?

' Well, my first tractor was one I used to drive for my father at Bradmore, before I came here. It was an old International, very difficult starting, but very useful, and it gradually took the place of horses. I used to bring a tractor over from Bradmore to do all the ploughing on this farm for several years before I came to live here.'

When did you start your herd of Guernseys?

'In 1954 I think it was. I went down to Cornwall to buy some young stock, and then we started a Guernsey herd. I started it, and I saw it ended as well. I gave up the milking herd about ten years ago [1991]. We had 80 milkers and 60 heifers, and sold them, fortunately before all the trouble with the dairy business. We were very sad to lose them.'

Can you tell us about the operation and the milk production?

' Well going back a long way, there was a Dairy College up at New Kingston, which is a mile away, and when my father was a boy here he used to take milk up there everyday. After they moved to Sutton Bonington, we had milk lorries coming round to collect the milk. We had it in seventeen gallon churns - which was jolly heavy - which we rolled! After that we had ten gallon churns, and after that of course we had refrigeration tanks. Getting very modern then of course. We were all TB tested, and all pedigree as well – the 'Kingbee Herd'. We had Guernseys, so we got extra money for the milk because of the quality. And that was good.'

'We grow different crops to what we used to do. We still grow wheat, barley and oats. We don't grow sugar beet any longer, we don't grow potatoes any longer. But we do grow oil seed rape now.'

(Norman Beeby)

'**I left** Kingston school on 31 Oct 1942 and started work the next day. I'd already got this job at the Midland Agricultural College, and I had to go up to see the farm manager on the Friday afternoon when I'd finished school. That were Mr Joe Blossom, and me dad said, "Tell him you'll start in the morning." I said, "What? Saturday?" He said "Aye." I said, "It's only half a day Saturday is." He said "It'll be like breaking a young horse in. You go for half a day Saturday, half a day Sunday, then you'll be fit ready for six o'clock Monday then." And that's what I did - six till six.'

' I got twenty eight shillings a week, and me mother said, "Well, how well you've done, boy." She said, "When me and your dad got married we'd got 18 shillings a week, and here you've got twenty-eight." She said, "I'll have a pound and you'll have eight shilling. But don't get spending all that eight shilling. Put some in the bank."
' When I first went, I was down at Manor Farm. Then, it was all hand milking, and I used to sit there and milk. There were forty six cows. There were a shed for twenty six, and two tens.'
' Tom Crann was in charge. There were two Cranns, Cyril Gibbins, Albert Bates, and me. I always remember the first cow in the shed called Golden Daisy. And old Albert Bates he used to get there first thing in the morning, and he'd do nothing. He'd never start to milk before anybody else, he always sat behind this cow smoking his old Woodbine there. Then, when everybody got there for six, he'd get up and he always milked this cow. And I said to Cyril Gibbins one day, "I wonder why old Albert always has that cow, he never lets anybody else have her?" He said, "Because it's easy milking." I said, "Oh!"

And then after a bit the milking machines went in and I said to old Tommy Crann, "Can I have a go at milking with a milking machine now?" He said, "No. You carry on hand milking." He said, "When you can do that properly you can machine milk." He said "You should milk nine cows an hour by hand, each man." I said, "Oh!" Of course to me it just depended how much milk they gave.

Then after about six months I went up to Sutton Bonington to the farm there. I've always been interested in horses since I was about five. I had whooping cough when I were about five or six, and Dr Jeffares said to me mother, "He wants to be outside in plenty of fresh air. That'll cure him." We were very pally with Bob Shaw, who was wagoner at Beeby's. And he said, "I'll have him with me Mrs Temple. Let him come with me," and I used to go to his house for seven in a mornin' and go out wi him with horses every day.

When I got tired he'd lift me on top and let me ride on one, and that was the start of the love of horses. Then I went up to Sutton Bonington and I worked on the horses there till they went in about 1953/54.'

'Old Bob Shaw died in March 1955. I think Norman Beeby had got two horses left, he'd got two greys.'

Were they still horse ploughing round the village when you were a boy?

' When the College took Manor Farm over - I think it was in 1939 - old Arthur Bramley, me mother's cousin, who lived in top Row, were working for Norton Garrett, that field where the Bull Farm is. It comes three quarters down Kingston and right up to the cross roads. That was thirty two acres. And he always used to say he ploughed thirty two acres with one pair of horses, for the valuation of the Manor Farm, in one month. They wouldn't want that today. Aye, that's what he always used to say it used to take; one month to plough it.'

' But most of the ploughing…when I started, they'd started using tractors. Beeby's did quite a lot of ploughing still with horses - Miss Beeby when she had Church Farm. But then of course when Norman came, he got a tractor you see, and he started ploughing with that. So old Bob didn't do so much horse ploughing. But at the College we used to do quite a lot … we drilled all the plot work with the horses. We drilled all the sugar beet, all the kale and the mangle. We did all the sowing with the horses, carting a lot of the sugar beet off, and muck carting. And we carted all the 'taters off with them. All them sort of jobs.'

(Ron Temple)

' **My** first employment was at the School of Agriculture at Sutton Bonington. I was 15. The first job I went into was on the pig farm. Charlie Culpin was the chap in charge. I worked under his supervision on pigs and learnt quite a lot – feeding, and helping the sows pigging as they went through the season.

I was on pigs for eighteen month to two year. Then I got a transfer down to Manor Farm at Kingston, which was the dairy farm at that time. The chap in charge down there was Cyril Gibbins. He was head cowman, and I actually worked with him. We did have a land girl come helping us, her first name was Daphne, but I couldn't say what her second name was. She used to come and help us out with the feeding and bedding.'

' My first weeks wages were 2 pounds 2 shillings and 10 pence halfpenny [£2.14p] for 48 hours. In fact, I don't think I shall ever forget that. When I compare some of the young lads at 16 today, what they're taking home….In them days the farming were good, but yer put a lot of hours in for the actual wages yer got. The farm wages was not very great at all in them days, and it was the late 1970s, 80s and 90s when the farm wages sort of picked up.'

Outside Manor Farm – 1940s (Mr.Musson & son on horses)

' The cow sheds themselves was like an L-shaped building. You come out the cow sheds into what they call the concrete yard, and the old dairy stood on one side of it at that time of day. I used to do quite a lot of hand-milking. The system was set up for air-milking, but as a young lad yer used to start off hand-milking, to get you into the hang of it. That was sitting on a 3-legged seat, actually sitting under the cow, and hand milking into a bucket. Although the air-line was in, there was still a lot being hand milked at that time.

Going off the hand-milking onto the air-line, you used to put the units on the cows, and if they was first milkers, you'd probably end up with a bucket with the unit smashed against the wall at the back of yer! 'Cos they regularly used to do that with being nervous.

The milk off each cow you used to take into the top of the churn itself. We used to call them little churns - what the suction units was fixed on - what yer used to put on the cows. Well yer used to have spare buckets, and while I'd gone to take that bucket of milk into the dairy, Cyril would put the top onto another bucket and onto another cow. That was more or less my job, to go back and forwards taking the milk while he was milking his self.'

' You used to go in the dairy and the old cooling unit used to be in a big steel frame. A three quarter tank on top of the steel frame - I'm not very tall - I used to stand on me tip toes to pour the milk over the top into it. It used to come down what they called a zig-zag water cooler. Then in the top of the churn there was a funnel with a cotton pad in the top of it, which the milk used to sieve through, in case there were any bits and that, come through. It was a pretty complicated set up really.

I think we were milking about 50 or 52 cows in them days.'

' My father was employed as a farm worker working for the Beeby's. There was a wagoner there, his name was Bob Shaw, he used to work the horses. As a lad, I used to come home from school at night, Kingston school, and go straight over to the stables – 'cos I like the horses – and go and spend a few hours with Bob in the stables. In later years as things went by, Norman swapped over on to tractors. Well I say tractors; his first tractor was a Fordson, one of the first Fordsons on spade-lug wheels that come out.

With Bob being wagoner, he was the first chap to get on the seat and have a drive on it. Bob's always been used to holding two reins in his hands behind an horse. He got on the seat, steering wheel in his hands, which he wasn't used to, and Norman stood behind on the draw bar. They put the tractor in motion to go up the field at the back of the farm, the middle field it was called, Bob was steering it, and they was heading towards the gate. Bob thought they were going to go straight through the gate and he started to pull on the steering wheel shouting "Woah! Woah!" He thought he was still behind the horse! Just before they got to the gate, Norman stopped the tractor. He put his foot on the brake, which was a brake and clutch in them days.'

(George Vickers)

Jack Beeby ploughing, Kingston Fields Farm

'**We** lived at Rempstone. That's where I first got involved with threshing and contracting, working for Beeby Brothers. I used to carry corn – apart from looking after the tackle – for £2 a day. Carrying the bags into the barn after we'd threshed, and they were 18 stones [c115 kilos] of wheat, 16 of oats, and 19 stone of beans.'

You were involved in harvesting in Kingston at Church Farm and Kingston Fields Farm?

'Yeah. I used to go both threshing and combining to Norman Beeby's. It'd be about 1960. Used to have good fun with the kids, get it [the corn] down to last bit and get the kids to catch the rabbits. That's when we were combining. Norman had said we could shoot rabbits off the combine, and sometimes we did carry a gun. I'd got a rack on me combine for a gun, if there were a fox or anything.'

' When we were threshing, we'd mostly get there set ready, day before - come over from Rempstone with the threshing tackle. That was tractor, drum and baler, sometimes a chaff cutter. The day started at half past seven - till five.

'Cos you'd got to get yer tackle right, yer drums had got to be level, scotched up, balers got to be in line else you were in trouble - belts coming off. It was hard work, but I seemed to enjoy it.'

How many men would be involved in the operation?

'Oh, there'd be two on the stack, one on the drum, one carrying bales, one needling the baler, another in the chaff hole. And probably two on the corn.

Everybody used to have followers, you know. Men used to follow yer for a days pay. Probably thirty bob [£1.50] or something like that, less than that perhaps. And they used to tramp behind – "Where you goin tomorrow? I'll be there."

We could do a bay of Normans in a day, a dutch barn bay. You could thresh one o' those in a day. You see at one time, when it was Ministry of Agriculture, they scheduled where you went, and you had to keep the corn going for the farmers, for the cattle. You perhaps did a day at Norman Beeby's, and then you were off to Kingston Fields, Elliots, all round you know.'

'I can remember once going to Kingston Fields. We stopped six days at John Lewis's and threshed them out there. It was mixed – wheat, oats and barley. I think the last time I threshed at Kingston Fields Farm was two stacks o' beans near the pump house.
' We moved on a Sunday to there, and there was over a foot o'snow on the ground. We left Rempstone on a tractor at 7 o'clock on Sunday morning, and got back at 8 o'clock at Sunday night.

I think we came to Kingston to do some steam cultivation in the fifties. I can't remember where, probably down the moor. I also went threshing at Firs and Oaks Farms. I think I was the last man to thresh for Lawrence Taylor before he died. That was across the road from the Oaks, in that dutch barn that is there now.'

'Mole ploughing. Well, you put a drain right across the bottom of the field - tile drains with gravel on top - say two foot, two foot six deep, and that 'ad got an outlet into a ditch or a brook. Then you went with a mole plough, and you moled holes up at every six foot centres, you know. And the steam engine stood at the opposite end of the field, and pulled mole plough through up to the engine. Then we pulled it back with a tractor, or another engine at other end, whichever was convenient. Same as steam ploughing. And it left a mole three and half…depending on what sort of expander you'd got on. It was a foot, like a round spike on a blade, and it went down into the ground, and the expander followed it. You could put whatever depth you wanted, or whatever size mole you wanted. It was quite successful in good clay ground. They stopped open for hundreds of years.'

this one was the first self–propelled combine, which was a Class SF combine. That was German. They were imported by Manns of Suffolk.

'And the first field we did wi' it, was on Kingston Fields Farm, on end o' Thrumpton Lane where you turn down to the Power Station. On the left - that field there. We did that one Saturday and Sunday. I should think that was around 1960.'

German CLAAS Combine, Kingston - 1960

Arthur Marshall with Case LA4 Tractor   c1950

'When we were contracting we had a special tractor, it was hand clutch. It was a Case LA4. It was sold at Beeby's sale a few years ago - same tractor - still running. It came from America. They come over in the war. I suppose they'd be on this Lend Lease job. We used that a lot at Kingston.

We also used a rather unique combine. When at Beeby Bros, we had three Massey Harris combines, and then along came this new one, and it was the first one in England which was self-propelled. There was trailer combines drawn by tractor, but

' When it was the old days, the old Massey Harris 726's, if we did 10 acre a day, we'd had a real good day. I think they used to charge thirty bob an acre, old money, and we'd had a good day. When the Claas come on the scene, I could do up to 20 acre a day, which was double the output. Good money, so it paid for itself in the extra time.

Well today, I mean you're talking 40-50 acres a day aren't you? You know, without any trouble, nobody gets offered a seat, and there's no bags. Yeah, it's a different life isn't it? '

(Arthur Marshall)

'**I remember** sometimes, when the cows came out of the sheds into the farmyard [Firs Farm], they'd come and look through the door of the house. There was three sizeable cow sheds and two loose boxes – no more than a couple of dozen cows. When I was very small there was one old horse left at the farm. It wasn't working, but they did have workhorses on the farm prior to that.

'My uncle Lawrence did the milking, probably David Fairweather would do some, and I think a Jack Blakeway from Kegworth, he milked at that time. Prior to that of course my mother had worked on the farm until we were born, she'd done the milking then. She'd be up very early doing it. I remember Mary Madeley working at some point on the farm, doing a bit of milking.'

'I recall an old wooden caravan with iron wheels which housed two Irishmen, Mick and Willy, they lived in there. They did hoeing of the sugar beet crops. We used to torment them a bit as kids, and one night we went round and put a wet sack over their chimney. They'd got a fire, and they came tearing out, really upset. They used to chase us. We we used to annoy and frighten them a bit, because they were very superstitious and believed in leprechauns. They'd tell us a lot of stories and we would kid them on about the leprechauns.'

(Carole Easom nee Taylor)

'**I can't** remember what age I was, ten, eleven, twelve or something like that, when they were potato picking. And they were short of the tractor driver. They sort of told me what to do, and I sat – oh, I remember this seat, oh it was hard! We had just a sack bag on it. But I'm sure the imprint was there for a long while after I'd got off!

Also, when we had threshing at the farm, [Kingston Fields] I remember Mr Peter Strutt. He was there in his working gear and he said, "I'll give you sixpence for every rat you kill, and three pence for every mouse." My word, my stick did do a lot of thrashing that day. I don't know how much I earned, but I'm sure it must have been a lot!'

(Christine Whitehead nee Joyce)

'**There** were about three horses that I can remember. Alf Middleton, he looked after them. He led them along and bridled and harnessed them up. But only one horse has stuck in my memory, and that was Peggy. I've got fond memories of being in the cart behind Peggy when we were fetching mangles out of the field, just as you go out of Kingston Fields Farm on the right hand side, and pulling the hay tedder.

I have fond memories of harvest time, stooking at night after they had been bindering. Collecting sheaves on top of the drays. Then in the winter months Beeby Brothers used to come threshing. Gino and me dad carrying the bags of corn up the loft. There were no fork lift trucks and tipping trailers then. I think it was 16 stone of wheat, 14 stone of barley, and they'd put them on an elevator thing, drop 'em on their back, and then carry them off up to the loft. It were absolutely incredible, the strength of them blokes in those days.'

'My sister Maureen and myself used to help in the dairy. At Kingston they used to make their own cream. My dad was milking on a Sunday afternoon. They used to cool the milk, then make the cream, and I think the cream, well most of it, all used to go up to the Hall in big containers. It was milk churns then, it wasn't automated.

We had all Jerseys, and a few Guernseys, and me dad used to show them at Kingston Show. I can remember him getting ready to go to the show in the cow shed - all the rosettes was up when they come back.'

' I think it was free housing, potatoes, and milk etc, off the farm. My father, when I was round about seven or eight, used to get about seven pound fifty, well seven pounds ten shillings, but I always understood that was fortnightly. It wasn't a lot of money.'

(Paul Winson)

'**My** dad was cowman at Kingston Fields. The cows were all named, and my dad used to name a lot of them. He was obviously not very imaginative because there was 'Heather – 1,2&3,' then 'Bluebell – 1,2&3,' and I don't know how many 'Daisys!' It was fantastic milk. He used to bring it in for breakfast, just warm, thick, creamy milk – very high in chlorestrol no doubt.

My father was a very quiet man, skilled in all he did at the farm. They didn't use the vet very often because they had their own remedies. He used to detest November when it was hedging and ditching time. I can still see him now, wrapped in hessian cloth to protect him, standing under this dripping hedgerow while he cleared it all out.'

'Another memory is riding on the seed drill with my dad. I remember he was saying how sad he was seeing all the rabbits with myxamotosis. It was quite new, something that was introduced, and he thought it was disgraceful.'

'One thing none of us were aware of at the time, and its something we can only be wise to in retrospect, is the huge changes we witnessed in agriculture. How we came from working the land at harvest time, particularly using the old baling systems and threshing machines, building stooks in the fields, and all the magic – magic for children at least – that that conjures up, to the changeover to combine-harvesters.

I used to love it when I came home from school and all these people were in the stackyard working away. My mum on the stack throwing sheaves down into the threshing-machine, my dad carrying the great big sacks of grain on his back. There were all manner of things going off. It was really rather exciting. I remember lots of rats about, and the dogs going absolutely mad after them.

When we brought the stooks back to the farm they had all the tractors working with trailers. I remember …Peggy, the Shire horse, we used to get her harnessed up in front of a trailer, and if Paul and I were able to ride on there, poor old Peggy used to fart away as she went merrily on her way! Of course, being children, we were just hysterical most of the time. She was a lovely old horse. Bless her. But I think its such a sad thing, because you obviously don't realise that you're witnessing something perhaps for the very last time.

And then of course the combine harvester came along, and that was exciting too for different reasons , watching the harvesters 'gollop' up the fields until there was one rectangle of corn left. There must have been hundreds of rabbits in this last few feet of standing grain, and most of them used to make a final dart for freedom, and again the dogs would be after them. It was bedlam really!'

'One very sad event that happened at the farm was when Peggy had an accident. She fell into a ditch and couldn't get out. Local men came and she had straps put round her and they pulled her out with a tractor. I think she died a little while later. We loved Peggy, she was a huge, monster of a horse, very docile, as Shire horses are. She was black and white, and had lovely white 'feathers' over her feet. She was an absolute stunner of a horse.'

(Maureen May nee Winson)

Kingston Fields, 1958 (David Winson on tractor)

'**I started** here [Kingston Fields Farm]in the July of 1963. I was paid £7 fourteen shillings (£7.70p) a fortnight.

There were six or seven farm workers at that time, something like that. We had a lot of cattle, so there was at least one tied up to them all the time. I remember Harry Brown and Ray Winson, as regards the animal side of it. There was Gino, the Italian chap, and Victorio, who was Gino's adopted son. There was quite a few other names that cropped up over the years, that have come and gone, but basically Gino and Victorio were the two that were here the longest. Alf Middleton, of course, was the horse man as much as anything. He used to keep them here. Alf, well he was a real nice chap. If you wanted to know anything about horses or anything like that, he was the man to talk to. He was a really steady chap.'

You hadn't still got horses down here at that time?

' We hadn't, no. Only Lord Belper's horses. He used to keep them here. The race horses and hunting horses and things like that. Alf used to be looking after them. But we didn't have any actual horses at all for working.

Crops were very similar to today. Most obviously wheat, which we still grow in a great amount. And barley. We used to grow oats, sugar beet, things like that, which we don't grow now.

We raised beasts for quite some time for fattening - for beef. Originally, we had suckle herds, and reared them up that way. The policy changed slightly - they bought calves in and hand-reared them, up till obviously they could look after themselves.

We went to a system of bigger machinery, therefore wanting bigger fields, so obviously certain hedge-rows and things disappeared. The staff was cut down a bit. Obviously with having bigger machinery you could get the work done with less people. Which is the way things go today. Probably we cut down a little bit on what we grew. The cattle went out altogether. Sometime in that period they phased cattle out. We had sheep as well, but they were also phased out. And we went to just purely arable. There's two of us now, and a summer helper, farming about 1500 acres.'

Do you have any regrets about changes that have been made on the Estate?

'No, 'cos I think that you grow with them. You don't, well I don't, look back on them and think, "Oh, I wish it was like that now." Not really, because I think that you live for today, or work for today, in that respect.'

(Leslie Joyce)

November Shoot, Kingston – 1933

From left: Walter Cox (underkeeper); Hon. Ronald Strutt (late 4th Lord Belper); David Cox, 77 year old keeper and loader; Algernon Henry, 3rd Lord Belper.

Albert Baxter (Born Sutton Bonington 1885, lived in Kingston from 1888) Gamekeeper at Etwall, Derbyshire (His brother Ernest Baxter married Lillian, David Cox's daughter)

Shooting Days

'the woods were driven out'

Pheasant Shoot – early 1960's. Head keeper Evan Joyce on right

' **I was** very keen. They had quite a big shoot and it was quite a thing, a couple of keepers, and people coming to beat. They had a team of guns who used to be invited, and they probably had a shoot every fortnight, usually on the Saturday so people could come and visit for a weekend. There were usually eight guns and they stood in a line, and the woods were driven out for the pheasants. Earlier in the season there were partridges that we shot at in the fields. I wasn't allowed to go to an important place, I went on the side. I enjoyed that very much.'

Did your father [3rd Lord Belper] also take place in the shoots?

'Oh yes, he was a very keen shot. He used to number people. You had a system of numbering to make it fair. So that you'd be number one for one drive, and then you'd move up to number three for the next, and so on, so that everybody got a best chance. But somehow it seemed to work out that my father was always in the best place, despite all those numbering systems to make it all very fair. He always had his very good share of the sport. But people didn't mind that, because he gave them a good day!'

'I remember people like the Duke of Portland from Welbeck, he came, and other grandees from round about, and quite a lot of other people who helped us.

Algernon Henry, 3rd Lord Belper – Nov. shoot, 1933

They didn't just ask the nobs, so to speak, they asked other people, particularly after the war. My father had a lot of contacts with people from Nottingham and so on, who had done good work in the war, and he would invite them to shoot as a sort of thank you for what they had done.'

What sort of bags did you have?

'Well in those days I think we used to get about two or three hundred, or something like that, but it was even done more extensively much earlier... because this was all after the war, and there was shortages of food. You couldn't rear very many birds because there wasn't the food available for them. So it was more restricted then. But in the early days, in the heyday of the big shoots in Edwardian times, they used to get very big bags. I think they got something like twelve hundred birds in one day, which nowadays would be very much frowned upon, not be a very good thing to do.'

(Hon.Peter Strutt)

Evan Joyce

Can you tell us about you father Evan Joyce, the late head gamekeeper?

'**He** came to the Estate in 1931, and he worked almost until he died in 1991. I should think it was about 1985 when he finished. He was very conscientious, worked seven days a week, and also out at night-time on poaching prevention. In 1987 he won a long service medal [for 65 years service]...well he wouldn't go, he was no good at that sort of thing. So I had to go to Chatsworth and receive it on his behalf.'

'Uncle Arthur was also a gamekeeper. He used to ride a bike, and when I used to see him coming I used to rush across the road and open this gate so that he didn't have to get off his bicycle. And he used to say, "Thank you my lad," and go off up the meadow.'

(Christine Whitehead nee Joyce)

Early 60s shoot. Under-keeper Shilton with stick

'**He** [my father] was what we would call now, one of the old school of gamekeepers. He lived for the job. It was a 365 day a year job...a dedicated man I suppose you might say.'

'I certainly went beating a few times. I enjoyed that. There were two under-keepers at one time, and then it was reduced to one, with Mr Trigg disappearing from the equation as it were.'

Can you recall a typical shoot in the 1950's?

'Pretty well tended in those days. There were a lot more beaters...and the guns were more landed gentry sort of people as to what they are now. Celebrities...such as Charlie Drake, people like that, used to come. It was a real good day – probably better than it is now. Bags were much bigger than now, a lot bigger. But they'd put a lot more into it then somehow. They didn't necessarily put any more pheasants down to be shot at, but they got more birds then – they were better shots, shall we put it that way.'

'Poachers? They used to have a fair few of them. I know they had a bit of a punch a time or two with sticks and the like. I think they were more intent on getting away! Poachers in them days were a bit less violent than what they are now. They've got a lot more determined.'

(Leslie Joyce)

'**My** brother Norman [Hogg] he used to help out with the beating, because when he left school he actually worked in Kingston Hall gardens. Father sometimes used to do it...they'd both go beating. Whatever they did, they used to get something to come home with. It might be a couple of rabbits. If they did really, really well they used to have a hare, you know. So that used to make a nice meal.'

(Dora Higgins nee Hogg)

'**I came** back from school – when they used to have the shoots from the Belpers at the Hall – to Kingston Fields Farm . My dad [Ray Winson] was a beater with all the men and the boys from the area. And I'm sure he hated it. He didn't like being a beater. I don't think he liked shooting for the sake of sport, but along he went without any say I suppose. He was being paid and that was the end of it.

This particular day I remember coming back to the farm and into the farmhouse, and there were no chairs. I don't know whether they were in Lewis's house, or in the barn, or the cowsheds, but they were being used for the shoot – to sit their precious bottoms on while they had some sort of meal.'

(Maureen May nee Winson)

Beaters & dogs take a break

'**Well**, shooting days at the Hall and shooting days now, are completely different. Because at the Hall we had the space whereby on the big days, they used to shoot double guns, and they always used to bring a man servant or gamekeeper with them, and they had to be given bedrooms. Well of course we'd got staff wings at the Hall, that was no problem, they also had to be fed, and of course the big ones [shooting parties] in the dining room. Once, we had a shoot that was let out to American's, and that was hilarious; forty seven people, who's luggage came from the airport, and they all had the same name. It was all the same family. And we had dinner parties for thirty four and thirty six, and you know it was completely different. The house was full, and the bells would go upstairs, and Aunty Peggy went to answer the bell and this American - they were husband and wife - were in bed after an exhausting day shooting, and they wanted a gin and tonic. Aunty Peggy was hysterical when she come down, she wasn't going to take them up she said, "They are in bed!" she said, "I'm not going to take them gin and tonic in bed." So I took it up. But the funniest thing was, they came for a week's shooting and they had seven evening shirts, and two shooting shirts. Guess who was washing shooting shirts after they'd gone out shooting? But on the last day they were... it was a Wednesday, and they were to go out to see his Lordship do the hunt, all with their brand new spanking video cameras you know - they were just coming out then - and I thought that they would go. But oh, no! The house that they were moving on to next, the lady of the house was going to the hairdressers. So she sent her staff over, took cars and vans to load all their luggage into... and I had to feed them. So instead of having three for lunch, I had forty nine! But never mind we got through!'

'Well the shoots, they've gone from....one week, it used to be a double gun shoot at the Hall - like I said it was very lavish - the next week, it used to be called the local shoot where his Lordship's local friends used to come. But there used to be no dinner party, it just used to be a luncheon party. Nowadays the shoot is syndicated, and his Lordship is a member of the syndicate. There are no dinner parties involved with it, and they only shoot single guns now. They come in and they have morning coffee, and lunch and afternoon tea. But then they go, they don't stay or anything like that.'

(Ann Millard)

Lord and Lady Belper stag hunting in Scotland

Ronald's two first Stags, Glenkingie 1926

The Midland Agricultural & Dairy College

'mostly making cheese and butter, and lectures'

Kingston Dairy Institute opened in 1895 on Lord Belper's Kingston Fields Farm, establishing a permanent Dairy School to serve Notts, Leics, Derbys and Lincolnshire. After expansion in 1900 it became known as The Midland Agricultural & Dairy Institute. Eventually instruction was transferred to Sutton Bonington, and in 1928 Kingston College closed.

The following extract is taken from the Journal (written in 1953) of a former student who attended the College in 1903-07.

'**At** this time I began to take an interest in Dairy work, and went on a course of Instruction to the County Agricultural College (at Kingston). I learned butter and cheese-making and was most interested in the latter.'

'[In 1905] I took up Dairy work again and had another year's course at the Agricultural College where I had a happy time & made many friends. There were about sixty men and women students in residence of all ages. Most of the men were studying Agriculture, just a few were in the Dairies with the women students.

The social side was well organised, Whist Drives, Dances & Concerts regularly arrayed during the winter months. Hockey for the women – I eventually became Captain of the Team – we played both at home and away, and thoroughly enjoyed it. In the Summer, cricket & tennis were played. I wasn't much good at the latter.'

(Ellen Turner, nee Smith, 1887-1953)

Ellen Smith - 1905

'**Coming** from a little village in Lincolnshire, [in 1924] I was nearly overwhelmed …In those days they ran dairy courses, which were called squeaker courses. It was for six weeks. I went on a six-week course to see if I liked it, and I liked it, so I decided to go on a longer course. It was nearly a days journey to get there. You'd to go from Carlton to Lincoln by train, then when you got to Lincoln you'd to go from Lincoln to Nottingham, and then from Nottingham to Kegworth. There were no telephones, nobody had a telephone…and my mother was so anxious, because I was an only child [aged 16], …and I've still got the telegram I sent her to say I'd got there safely.'

Nancy Speed in 1926

Can you tell us about your accommodation; I understand you stayed in a Hostel on West Leake Lane?

'Very primitive. I can't remember an awful lot about it, but we did each have a room of our own, but they were very, very small. I think we'd about one bathroom between eleven of us. There were some rooms downstairs, including a common room, and Miss Annie Pritchard, the Dairy Instructress at the College was in charge of that hostel. I can't remember whether we'd any hot water, but there was a tap at the top of the stairs, and we used to fetch water in a jug. I think we had a basin in our bedroom, it was very primitive. We didn't have a bath very often!'

MADC group (Saxilby, Speed, Lamb) **Kingston - 1925**

'We had a special uniform. Cotton dresses, pink and white stripes, and white cap with a big starched front, but only when we were working in the Dairy. Not when we went to lectures.'

'Mr Stafford, he was a character. "Now girls. Now girls!" he used to come in, "Now girls. Now girls!" He was a wonderful man, very knowledgeable on dairying, but he wasn't the best of lecturers. He lived just near.'

'Some of the neighbouring farmers used to bring the milk in, then some of it was separated for cream to make butter, and some went into cheese making. We used to make cheese in different rooms in the College; one was the butter room; one was the cheese room. We made all sorts of cheese, all varieties. And one of the things I remember, Mr Stafford was an ex-Army man, and at Armistice we always had the two minutes silence in one of the lecture rooms. He was very keen on that.'

The Hostel on West Leake Lane, about 1907

Do you recall any student pranks?

'We didn't do anything wrong. I remember once, lads, they all lived at Sutton, they came and invaded the hostel one night. Poor Miss Pritchard, she locked herself in her bedroom, in her room, because she couldn't cope. And they ransacked that hostel… We tried to keep them away, we girls, and I tell you there was a tap on the top of the landing, and we kept throwing water on these lads to deter them!'

(Nancy Speed)

'**I lived** down in Hertfordshire…I went up there by motorcycle. I lived at Kingston at the College…Well, it was a new experience for me. I went straight from home. The first year, [1925] I went as a farm pupil at the Dairy College.'

Can you tell us about your dairying course?

'Well, mostly making cheese and butter, and lectures. The course was a supplementary course to the agricultural course, to go with a DD (Dairy Diploma). Normally it takes longer, but as I was doing an agricultural course so many of the subjects were the same, and so I didn't have to take them.'

What do you remember about your College days?

'I think I remember most about cheese making. There were great big vats you know, and the girls in those days - it was disgusting, but they used to stir it all by hand - and round the vat you'd have two or three boys, two or three girls. They had bare arms, no gloves or anything, and they used to stir milk up by hand. And of course we used to play with the girl opposite under the milk! You see we had about half a dozen people, and you stirred underneath. No question of proper tools or anything, very primitive.

And the other thing I remember, we made Stilton at the end of the season. I was allowed to make one of my own during the year, and put it in the place to cure so it would be ripe for Christmas. I then took it home. I remember it was my father's favourite cheese, he loved it. It was about this tall, a round one. I don't know what it weighed, I should think about five or six pounds.'

'We used to pack it by hand, the curd, take a handful and pack it into a long container – the mould. You did it very carefully, leaving plenty of air. You see it's one of the few cheeses that's not pressed. It's all pressure now, mainly. Stilton, you had it not too wet - and it's self draining. But the other cheeses of course, you had a screw-up press.'

'I was really keen on sports. I played hockey, mixed hockey, in those days. There were local teams in the villages all around.'

'J.G.W.Stafford? Yes, 'Daddy' we used to call him. I remember he was a very busy chap, very conscientious. Great deal of energy.'

(John Benson)

'**A few** memories of my father, J.G.W. Stafford : He got the name "Daddy," used by many students, because my two older brothers used to run over to the dairy at Kingston calling, "Where's my Daddy?

MADC Hockey Club, 1926 (John Benson on left)

Stilton Cheese-making Room at Kingston

Where's my Daddy?" Dad was very much a father figure to the many he helped, a very thoughtful and kind man. He and my mother provided a 'home from home' for many lonely souls (often foreign students). Sing-a-longs around our piano - usually played by a student - were very popular. Daddy played the violin or cello.'

' I remember 'Kitty', my brother Owen's pony, which he used to ride to Kingston School. He was allowed to tether it in the park next to the school playground, then he would ride it home. He would sometimes ride his pony with Lavinia Strutt (later Duchess of Norfolk). 'Kitty' was also family transport, pulling a trap, which we continued to use even after we moved to Kegworth in 1932.

Dad was a clever man, and an excellent teacher. He was always willing to pass on his knowledge. Water was H_2O to us! Cleanliness in milk production, from the cow shed to the table, was very important. He was really strict about this. He judged cheese and butter at the dairy show in London each October, also at many shows around England, and in Ireland and Wales.'

'JGW was a keen horseman, rode well, and taught all of us to ride at an early age. He loved music, and I loved singing with him at Weslyan Chapel (at Kegworth). We, (Owen, Dennis and myself) were very fortunate to have such wonderful parents.'

(Doris Henson nee Stafford)

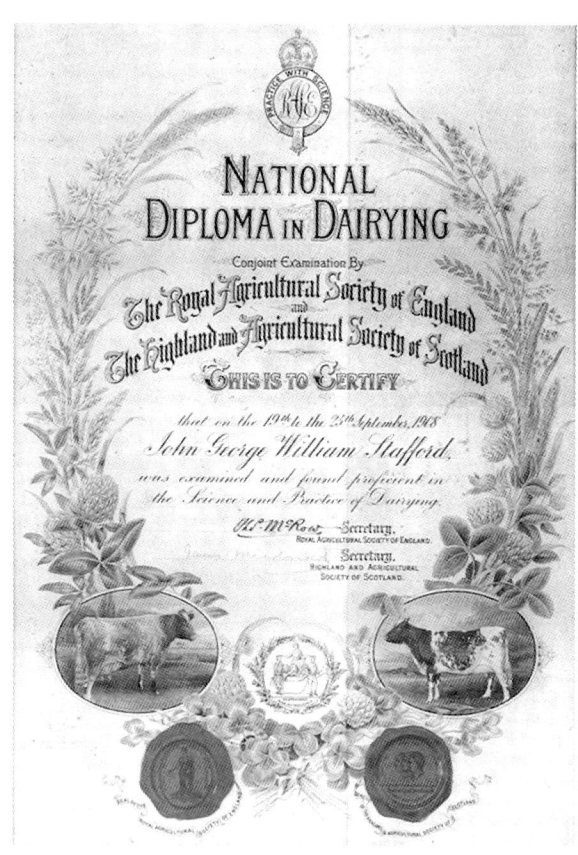

Dairying Certificate awarded to J.G.W.Stafford whilst a student at Kingston - 1908

J. G. W. Stafford

Cheese-making Room – Kingston. c1925

The Fine Art Company

'It was a happy little pastime'

This rural craft workshop, started in the late 1920s by Harry Woodfield, manager of Kingston Gypsum Mine, was situated in a building at Kingston Fields Farm and employed local people. Large blocks of gypsum – raw material of alabaster – were brought from the mine on the estate to the workshop. It closed down at the onset of World War II.

Former Dairy College buildings – showing site of Fine Art Company to the right

'My father (Harry Woodfield) was so interested in gypsum and alabaster, and there was an obvious little market for decorative ornaments, that he decided to start this little Fine Art industry down in one of the cottages at New Kingston. He employed a man called Mr Lomas, who used to come over from Derby in his little Austin, bull-nosed Swallow Austin 7, to look after the business. We used to turn out decorative things like lamp bowls, ash trays, book ends, and the like. The one piece-de-resistance of that little industry was a font made up of a baby lying on its back with it's knees up, and arms up as well, and the bowl resting on the knees and hands. It was a tremendous lot of care and attention went into it, to try and produce the same colour in alabaster as the baby's skin. I can't tell you where it is now, but it did I believe, go into a church somewhere in the north of the County. That was in the late 20s, early 30s. Unfortunately, the industry had to close down because the Italians were importing cheap, dyed alabaster ornaments at a much reduced price than we were selling them at. Ours was purely a hobby; and we didn't make a profit, as long as we covered our expenses. It was a happy little pastime.'

'How many were employed? Oh, not many, just a mere handful. Most of it was hand made. There would have been the odd lathe of course to turn circular objects like lampshades, candlesticks and such like, but nothing much more. It was just one room with a lot of benches, and people working at them...and a lot of alabaster about.'

(Richard Woodfield)

'They had a big space [in] a building next door to where Mr Lewis the farm bailiff lived. And they had a few staff, mostly women I think, who, out of the gypsum, made these rather charming things – various bowls, ashtrays, globes for lights, and so on. That was quite a big business. I remember going in there and seeing ...ladies in white overalls and handkerchiefs on their heads, because it was a bit dusty.'

(The Hon. Peter Strutt)

'**They** used to bring it [gypsum] down in big blocks from Kingston Mine, and saw it and machine it into little things - ashtrays, candlesticks, even beads. Some of the big ones were lamps, globes you know…chandelier things. The biggest I saw was about two foot across. But they cost the earth they did - a little string of beads was two guineas, which was a fortune in them days.'

'I remember, I once went and had a look through the window, and I saw the diamond studded saw that they cut the blocks up with.'

(George Smith)

'**We've** got a few pieces that were made there, ashtrays, and lights – you know, the big globe that you had in the middle of your ceiling. That's the sort of thing I've got, and a necklace and paper knife - all belonged to my parents and no doubt were given as presents to them.'

(Christine Whitehead)

'**We** have a little bowl from the Fine Art Company. It was mum that bought it from the showroom there It would have cost – not a lot – about 5/- (25p) or something like that.'

(Muriel Allen nee Brownlow)

Items made by the Fine Art Company

Skating on the Lake

'it was heaven, it really was'

The following extract is taken from the Journal (written in 1953) of a former student at Kingston Dairy Institute in 1903-07.

'**Year** 1906: It was a hard winter, and we were allowed to skate on the lake in Kingston Park, owned by Lord Belper, by moonlight. This was the only time I had the chance to practise skating. I remember sending home for my mother's skates, which she had kept safely from being a girl.'

(Ellen Turner nee Smith, 1887-1953)

' **One** year the lake froze over and they put lanterns and lights up – the people from the Hall did – and they'd got this …I suppose it was a kind of ice-chair [gondola] or something, and they were giving people rides. You could go on it.
  People came from all round skating, those that could skate or slide. Everybody was so friendly. I don't know whether the actual Belpers were there, but they put all these different lights – they'd be like storm lanterns. And somebody had even got some music and….it was really fantastic!'

(Muriel Allen nee Brownlow)

'**It seemed** in those days we used to have much harder frosts, and crueller winters than now. Anyway, I remember it being frozen over two or three times completely. Because its quite a large surface area and we used to play rather amateurish ice hockey on the lake. Then there was always a bit of a panic when you'd hear the ice sort of cracking. But a lot of people said "Oh, that's a very good sign. Its not going to cave in," but I didn't really believe that.'

'But we had a lot of fun, both men and women, and children, and we sort of picked up Kegworth and Kingston and that sort of thing. We played inter-village matches. But I mean very, very rough. Nothing formalised. It was just very good fun. I can remember those cold afternoons, with the light going down and the darkness setting in, and it was very eerie and cold. You don't get that now very much.'

(Hon. Peter Strutt)

'**We** skated on the lake in 1941 and 42. That went on for weeks. I had no skates with me but there was somebody called Sally Lunn, of all names, who lent me hers. The boys came out. Nobody said they shouldn't be there or anything, and the lake was just....whenever there was free time, it was skating. Day after day after day, I've got it in my diary, all the weeks.'

Was this all the students from Midland Agricultural College?

'Yes. They wouldn't have come normally, so I would think the Belper's must have said, "Let them come." But it was heaven, it really was! But our difficulty was, we were supposed to be working at the College, and you couldn't cycle – you know they'd so much snow you couldn't cycle from Kingston to Sutton Bonington.'

(Joan Johnson nee Donnell)

Extracts from Joan's Diaries :

19 Jan 1941 – Cold   *Di, Enid, Clare, Jean & I went to Kingston Lake to see the skating. Jean had skates & soon all of us had borrowed some. Mrs Rowe lent me hers. Brushed a rink & shovelled away snow.*

11 Jan 1942 – Freezing cold   *Went sliding on ice with Titch & Arthur Asher etc. Later borrowed skates!!! Oooh.*

12 Jan 1942 – Very cold   *After a whopping tea we went skating on the lake at Kingston.*

16 Jan 1942 – Frosty   *Worked at Dig for Victory plan with Pauline. To Kingston for Mr Rowe's demonstration. Skated on lake before tea.*

17 Jan 1942 – Freezing cold   *Worked at Dig for Victory plan. Then skated on Kingston lake till 5 o'clock. Tea of cocoa & syrup. Hop till late.*

18 Jan 1942 – Slight fall of snow   *Saw AA about skating & met him on the ice plus skates. Tried turns, played tig & hockey & thoroughly enjoyed ourselves.*

Extracts from 1945 MAC Magazine :

23 Jan. Skating on Kingston Lake – ice firm but it cracked a bit – "ffortescue" showed his prowess, we were much impressed.

Extract from 1946 MAC Magazine :

19 Jan. Lord Belper gives us permission to skate on Kingston Lake.

20 Jan. Joe finds a soft spot on the ice.

' **We** used to go there at night time. The College students from the Agricultural College at Sutton Bonington used to come down, and put their cars round the outside of the lake and switch their headlights on so it was all lit up across the ice. They'd be skating and we'd be sliding, the lads out the village. There was one or two nasty experiences. Some of the students got a bit too close to the waterfall end, and the ice broke away one night and in a couple of them went. They got 'em out all right, but they'd be a bit uncomfortable. Them lads they used to take chances. They'd dare each other to who could get the closest to them sort of places. Otherwise it were marvellous really.'

' One student lad come up with the idea of trying to ride a bike on the ice. He come on with this bike one night; no tyres on it, just the bare wheels…he got so far out, and bang went the bike underneath him. He tried it two or three times, and gev it up as a bad job in the end and chucked it back on the grass. Otherwise there was some good nights, and it were quite enjoyable the skating on it.'

(George Vickers)

Kingston Hall Lake

SKATING ON THE ICE.

World War II Years

'a very spartan time'

The Green & cottages – 1940 (Note white painted kerbs to assist drivers during the blackout)

'**During** the war of course….everything was rationed. The clothes were rationed, the food was rationed, and the petrol was rationed, and it was a very spartan time. We were encouraged to grow as much as we possibly could and given financial incentives to do so, because we had to keep the nation fed as best we could - because of the German blockade. It was all manual work of course in those days. There wasn't a lot of mechanisation as there is today.'

'We had evacuees from London for a short while, a mother and daughter, actually in the house we were living in then. And we had German prisoners during the war to do threshing and sugar beating. Land girls as well, because there was a hostel at Bunny. The German prisoners of war came from a prison of war camp near Loughborough.'

' We had some very good auctions for the war effort, where people gave things, and then they were auctioned by Lord Belper. And people paid silly money because it was for the war effort. But when you've got two people bidding against one another the article would probably fetch a hundred times what it was worth. But it was all in War Bonds.'

(Norman Beeby)

'**He** [Harry Woodfield] was one of a team of A.R.P. wardens for an area on the Basford Rural District Council, and he was a Basford Councillor as well. We had a special phone fitted in the house, and whenever there were any air raid warnings around Derby, Nottingham, Leicester or locally, he used to be telephoned in the middle of the night. He had to then ring the one warden that was supposed to be on duty, to get him up and get him out. Or, if it was his turn, then he had to get up and go out.'

And did we have any air raids?

'Not any nearer than the big towns and cities around us. There were some bombs dropped across the Park on Kingston Estate. That was very soon after the War had started. Because the Belper's had always had a house party for Kingston Show - the Annual Show which took place on August Bank Holiday Monday - and at the last one, [in 1939] one of the house guests on that occasion was the German Ambassador, a lady. We always thought that the bombs that did drop in and around Kingston were of her doing. Whether she was trying to get the Gypsum Works or the Hall, we didn't know.'

(Richard Woodfield)

'**I remember** when the sirens went, we all used to go up to Lord Belper's place and go down the cellars. We all had masks on…but we could take them off when we got down the cellars. We had to walk to start with, but then we started to run if we thought anything was going to happen.'

'I remember where they [the bombs] fell out in the park and later on, after the war they planted trees [there].'

' You couldn't get a lot of food in those days but we never went without. Mum must have been very good at that.'

'We used to knit squares for blankets at school and…used to knit those things for soldiers, the helmets [balaclavas]..in khaki wool.'

(Sylvia Church nee Joyce)

'**Whenever** there was an air raid we used to go and sit on the stairs, on the bottom three steps, away from the windows, and I remember old Mrs Chadbourn from up the road used to come down [to the Lodge] every time. She'd have about four or five coats on! I remember her coming down [West Leake Lane] there, and she used to come and sit on the stairs with us. Then her son used to come and fetch her back after the raid had finished.'

'I can't remember Land Girls, but we had prisoners. First of all it was the German's, two of them, Willy and Ernst. They lived in a room at the farm. [Kingston Fields] My parents invited them over to our home, and used to make them feel at home, giving them meals and tea and cake and things, and they were very appreciative really. They were really nice gentlemen, and they stayed friends for many years, even after they'd gone back to Germany. Then there were the Italians; that was Gino and Bolo. They did the same really, they used to come across to the house and everything, and we were all great friends. Gino, after he went back to Italy, brought his wife Adelma back and came to live at Kingston, and stayed there for many years until his death in about 1992.'

' First of all they used to go back each night in a bus…to somewhere in Nottingham or Derby, a camp I expect. I always remember their jackets, they'd got a big round ring of different coloured material in the middle of the back, so I suppose they were easily spotted.

But afterwards they lived round the back of the farm in a big room there with - I remember - the big stove in the corner; one of these iron stoves to keep them warm, and two single beds. And they'd got Rosaries hung up on the wall behind their beds. But I think they were happy enough, because everybody treated them very well, and they were good workers.'

Rupert Strutt & Lady Belper - 1939

'Lady Belper very often used to come down [to the Lodge]. Once, I don't know whether it was the Women's Voluntary Service, she was on duty in Leicester in the blitz - you know the air raids. She came back one morning and brought a little black kitten that she'd found on this burning roof, and she called it 'Blitz' and gave it to us.'

(Christine Whitehead nee Joyce)

'**We** had a [evacuee] mother and a baby girl. They came from London and they stayed with us, well I should think about six to nine months, but then went back to London. They found the country life a bit quiet.'

'Soldiers hired the Village Hall out during the war. Events were also held there in aid of prisoners of war to raise money for food parcels.'

(Mary Beeby)

'**George** dug a big air-raid shelter...at the top of the garden, and when there was an air-raid, we used to go and get in. And he lined it with (railway) sleepers I think. And one night we had a bomb drop in the park - the back park - and Uncle Jack was standing outside the shelter to see what was happening, and a bit of shrapnel fell down against him off the bomb. But before we had the shelter I used to go in next-door, and we used to get under the kitchen table. Grandad Smith used to say, "Come on Vera, lets have you under the table!" And of course we used to go under the stairs in here, before George made the shelter. But he (George) was always at work while all this was going on. He used to work such long hours.'

'We had a field across from the house with two big elm trees in, and we used to go in there, and sit and do our knitting. And they had a horse called Peggy...and when George was on nights during the war and I was on my own, if I could hear Peggy knocking about under the tree, I used to feel safe. Although it's a silly thing to say. But I always used to listen for her knocking about. That's all gone now, its all ploughed up.'

(Vera Smith)

'**I remember** evacuees at the school...there was two girls used to be at Mr Smith's at New Kingston, one was named Pauline and one named Beryl, I could be wrong. Then there was Kathleen and Douglas Willey at Marshall's farm, [Oaks] on the top road.'

Kathleen and Doug they was from Sheffield. I knew their mother was a nurse, and her father was in the forces at the time; I can remember because poor old Dougie used to get into trouble nearly every day with Mrs Foster.'

'If ever he did anything wrong, she would get the stick out to him, and it was so many on each hand. But then as time went on he used to take the stick off her and he'd break it. So then she would send him out to get another one from the spinney next to the school, and he'd got to have the right thickness. He'd bring two or three in, and it would not have to be too thick or too thin, just right. Later on still he decided he'd had enough of that, and he used to chase her round the classroom with it!'

(Dora Higgins nee Hogg)

'**I joined** the Coldstream Guards, [in 1942] - because my brother Ronald was also in the Guards - when I was eighteen. We had about a year training, and then joined the Guard's armoured division which was tanks and infantry, and I was in an infantry battalion. I wouldn't have liked to have gone in a tank – we sometimes rode on the tanks but I wouldn't like to be in one. So I was in the army about five years.'

Nevertheless you made a bit of a name for yourself. You rose to the rank of Captain and were awarded the Military Medal?

'That's right. I think anybody else would have done the same as I did in the circumstances. But I wanted to stay in the army. It was very worrying and quite frightening in the war. I enjoyed the army very much, it was a very good sort of club, very good morale. It was a good thing to be on the winning side so to speak, not retreating but advancing all the time into Germany.'

'When the war was finished, I got leave and I came back, and my parents drove in the car to fetch me from Loughborough Station. Going up the hill towards the lodge gates near the drive of Kingston [Hall], my father started tooting the horn, and I couldn't understand why he was doing that. But he was just warning the people at the top by the gates who came down to greet me. Also, some sort of ritual they had was meant to be a great honour. They tied ropes onto the car and pulled the car with me sitting there in it. At first I was rather embarrassed, but then it was really rather fun, and I just had to be careful when they got up a bit of speed to steer it promptly, so I didn't run anybody down. But I always remember that as something that happened.'

(Hon. Peter Strutt)

MAYOR OF LOUGHBOROUGH'S WAR FUND

A GRAND VARIETY ENTERTAINMENT
BY THE
'KINGSTON FOLLIES'
In aid of the Mayor's Comforts Fund in the
TOWN HALL, ————LOUGHBOROUGH.
WEDNESDAY, MAY 1st, 1940
PROGRAMME CONSISTS OF CONCERTED ITEMS, HUMOROUS AND CHARACTER SKETCHES, etc., etc.
Doors Open 7 p.m.   Commence 7.30 p.m.
ADMISSION : 1/6, 1/- and 6d.
Come and Support this Worthy Object.
— A CURE FOR BLACK-OUT BLUES. —
Tickets may be obtained at the Loughborough Public Library.

Under the Co-operative Fruit Preservation Scheme (sponsored by the Ministry of Food), the Kingston Women's Institute have made over 1,000 lb. of jam from fruit picked earlier in the year. In the picture Lady Belper (third from right), who is president of the Institute, and chairman of the jam depot, is seen, with members, putting covers on the jars at the preserving centre at Kingston Hall, ready for distribution to shops for sale.

'**My** mother helped in the village quite a lot. She was keen on the W.I. and the church. During the war the Women's Institute – I can't remember how many times they went – but in the fruit time they used to go up to the Hall and make jam and sell it. And Lady Belper and all of them were there in the kitchen.'

(Ron Temple)

'**When** the war was on me mother had a jam kitchen up at the College [Sutton Bonington]. Lady Belper used to go and help her. They used to can fruit – all the fruit out the gardens.

I can remember Michael Strutt being killed in the war, and being buried at Kingston, remember going to the funeral. One or two of the lads were killed in the war that went to school with me. Roy Hall, he went down with the first ship sunk – The Oak, at the beginning of the war. Then Ivan Hill - he was in the airforce - was killed a week after Michael Strutt.'

(Ethel Cook nee Marshall)

Kingston Bridge in 1940s

Because of the large influx of student evacuees at the Midland Agricultural & Dairy College at Sutton Bonington, the College had to arrange further outside accommodation – *"Lord Belper very kindly came to the rescue in providing accommodation for 14 people on the top floor of Kingston Hall."*

(The Kingstonian, MADC Magazine, 1942)

'When war broke out I was already booked to go to Swanley Horticultural College in Kent. We were only there about two terms, when the bombing got so bad, I mean Swanley was really in the path of the planes, that we were evacuated to Midland Agricultural College at Sutton Bonington, and I was there for the rest of my three year course, 1940 - 1942.'

Joan Donnell - 1941

'At Midland, they were getting short of room, and the degree students and a few of us diploma students, were allowed the flat over the top of Kingston Hall. It was quite separate from the main house, but already the previous years we were using Kingston Hall for our practical horticulture. Leslie Rowe and his staff, Percy Dolman and Jack Bones in the glass houses, they had been giving us practical work, like potting up chrysanthemums... or lifting a herbaceous border and putting it back. This was part of our practical work for our diploma in horticulture, so we'd already been going to Kingston.'

Can you remember what your accommodation was like?

'Well, it was simply glorious after some of the digs I'd been in. It was a very large room overlooking the grounds and the lake, shared with only one other girl, a degree student. And we had a common room where they lit us a fire; and because no doubt we were older students they did allow us to entertain there, but not after ten o'clock. It was an ideal situation. We did not have meals there, only at the weekends, and then it was the sort of meal you could bring down like tea... there was no cooking done for us. We had to go back to the Midland College for all our meals. But we worked hard there, we not only were taught to do things, we also helped them do a lot of work. I learned the names of all my shrubs down there. It was a lovely long shrub border, and I still know them from that time.'

'Leslie Rowe was a gentleman. Percy [Dolman] was the outdoor man. You see most of them must have gone by then – been called up – in fact Jack Bones left in 1942 to be called up.'

'We didn't mix in the Hall. The only time we really got into the Hall, because our flat was entirely separate, and you went up big stone steps into it, was when Constance Spry, a famous flower arranger and cookery writer, came for a whole week and took us students at the Hall for arranging flowers. Then Lady Belper was quite glad to receive these arrangements through her house. I thought Constance Spry was very clever. She said to each of us, "Divide into two's," and she gave each of us a colour - yellow, purple and so on. And she said, "Don't despise the odd bit of vegetable, you know," and so we'd go out over the grounds picking up our colour, and it was amazing how bits of beetroot leaf came in with purple asters. She just told us to go and get colour, not to be snobbish about it and get a bit of heliotrope, but to go out and get whatever colour we had. And it worked marvellously!

And these arrangements were then taken into the house. So I really saw over the house then. Little Constance Spry was no bigger than myself, about five foot nothing. She had all these bangles and when her arms went up they went 'tinkle, tinkle, tinkle, tinkle', you know. She was a wonderful character. But when she got into the main sitting room and was putting this thing on the piano, she saw that the Duke of Norfolk's wedding photographs were displayed. And she got really excited. "I did the flowers for the Duke of Norfolk, you know," and there you could see all her arrangements in the photographs. She was thrilled to bits! That was the late Lavinia Strutt that married the Duke of Norfolk. I'll never forget Constance Spry's delight.'

'We often saw Lord Belper if we'd been clearing the herbaceous border. If there was a lot of rubbish to burn he would instigate a bonfire...he just loved them. He also pottered about, and when we were working he'd come and have a look. And his son came once.'

'My most enduring memories? I think being out at Kingston Hall as a student...and as I say the sitting room, a glorious sitting room with a fire. Can you imagine, in war time? We were spoilt. I was very sad leaving, I'd had a wonderful time.'

(Joan Johnson nee Donnell)

Extracts from the wartime Diaries of Miss Ethel Joan Donnell

Miss Donnell was billeted in 1940 at MADC, Sutton Bonington. From Sept 1941 to June 1942 she occupied an apartment at Kingston Hall. Her diaries provide a fascinating insight of what it was like to be an evacuee horticultural student in wartime.

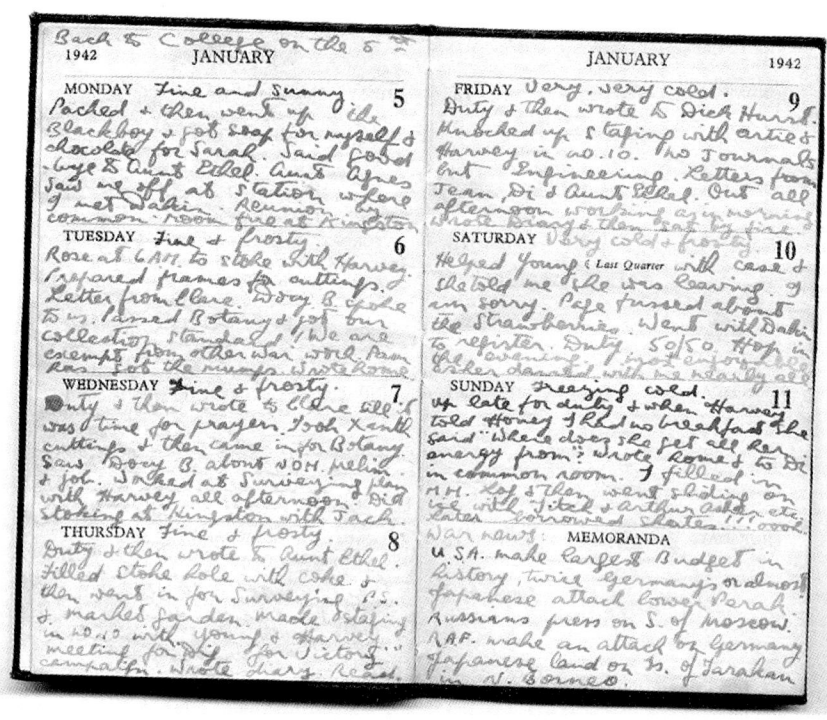

Tues 7 Jan 1941 - *Thaw.*
(War in Africa progressing favourably)

Cycled on snow packed roads to Kingston. Cut back Laurels with Mr Rowe and Percy & burnt branches. Lord Belper & son helped us in the afternoon.

Fri 10 Jan 1941 - *Very wet.*
(Big RAF raid on Calais)

Interesting Botany lecture on Fern reproduction.. Then to Kingston Hall where Mr Rowe took me into the house to help Jack with the flowers. The Hon.Peter Strutt was feeding his fish in the scullery. I saw into the Living Rooms. Jack in good humour. Took Carnation cuttings in the afternoon & he told me Mr Rowe had said I was the best in the group. Deep blushes!

Thur 23 Jan 1941 - *Frosty*
(Tobruk captured)

The road to Kingston was very dangerous. I fell off at gate & Clare too. Jean, Enid, Clare & I emptied out old 'chrysant roots' & took cuttings to send home. Worked hard to get a 'posh' job which turned out to be building a hot bed. My curls came out in the mist.

Mon 9 Jun 1941 - *Cloudy & wet*
(Cyprus ready for air invasion)

Jean in Plant house at Kingston.. Watched her & Jack thin grapes. Back to Kingston to see shrubs in flower with Jean & Margot.. Chased sheep out of garden for Lady B & saw Duchess of Norfolk.

Sat 27 Sept 1941 - *Very wet*
(Odessa & Leningrad fight back)

Learnt that 3rd years are to sleep at Kingston Hall NOT College.

Sun 19 Oct 1941

After lunch we cycled to Ratcliffe & left the weeks washing, went to Thrumpton & Barton & called for last weeks on way back. Ate apples all the way.

Mon 27 Oct 1941 - *Cold & dry*

Had Lord & Lady Belper & friend to supper.

Wed 19 Nov 1941 - *Wet*
(Enemy tanks thrust
N & S of Moscow)

Played Hockey after dinner in mixed match. Good game! To Kingston & celebrated Cabbage's 21st Birthday with huge party with eats & lots of singing. Lordy interrupted us at 11.45!

Wed 10 Dec 1941 - *Fine but cold*
(Russians recapture Rostov)

Huge tea at Kingston & then patched my breeches after washing.

Thurs 11 Dec 1941 - *Fine & mild*
(Germany & Italy declare
War on USA)

Changed, for coffee downstairs with Lord & Lady B. Played game. Small & Titch gave rendering of sketch.

Fri 12 Dec 1941 - *Stormy*

Belpers away on Friday so we sang Carols in their Library and had coffee.

Wed 28 Jan 1942 – *Very cold & wet*

I had to go to Loughborough to stage Window for Dig for Victory. Went in College van with Hemp & Pauline. Met Arthur at 5 & saw "Billy the Kid" at the Odeon.

Thur 29 Jan 1942

Excavated for frames with the Womens Land Army & Burrows. To Loughborough with Cabbage to sit in Boots in Advisory capacity for Dig for Victory campaign. Only one question asked!!

Sat 31 Jan 1942 - *Very cold & frosty*

Got celery with Land Army girl & they helped on French garden. Wrote Diary at the Common room fire Kingston. Changed to blue frock & jacket & went to Hop with Titch & Small. Had heaps of partners.

Sun 1 Feb 1942 - *Heavy snow*

Cycled thro' snow back to Kingston & remade old gloves out of extinct stockings. Tea of egg paste, milk & milk. Then rehearsed for Variety in which I'm the Russian Rose.

Tues 24 Mar 1942 - *Fine*

Saw Arthur after dinner. Prepared for Dance to which we expected the RAF band but it did not come. Half Home Guard called out.

Sun 17 May 1942 - *Sunny periods*

Lay in bed until after 10am. Mended clothes & played the Gramophone. Took washing to Ratcliffe. Got boat on lake & ate sandwiches with 2 Jeans & Pilkie.

Thur 18 June 1942

To Kingston where we talked about the women's place after marriage.

Sun 21 June 1942 - *Sunny & warm*

Dick & Arthur came to tea at Kingston & went out in the punt after. Simply grand!!

GYMKHANA IN AID OF GOTHAM CHURCH FUND
HELD AT KINGSTON. MAY 1929

Lady Belper with Peter and Lavinia Strutt

Kingston Show

'Kingston's day of glory'

The first Kingston Show – formerly known as the Kingston & West Leake Flower Show – took place in 1888 in a corner of the Park. About 1900 the show combined with the Kingston Shire Horse Society Show, which up until then had been a separate show held in October. With breaks only for the two World Wars, and foot & mouth in 1952, the larger show continued until its closure in 1965.

Kingston Show with Hall and terrace - 1930

'**Kingston** Show started in it's very early days as a flower show, and father [Harry Woodfield] took over the Secretaryship in 1922. He wasn't a very happy man on the first day. He made a loss because all the parkland in front of Kingston Hall where the show was held was under water, as was the village as well. So we didn't do very well on that occasion. But the show built up over the years, and it was held every year on August Bank Holiday Monday. It was the first Monday in August in those days, and not the last as it is now. It built up to be a very popular show and a real happy family day out. I think the crowds used to well exceed twenty thousand, and in the end we had well known horse people like Ted Williams and Pat Smythe. We had to conform to the British B.S.J.A. rules and have all the correct jumps, which cost the show people quite a lot of money at the time. But it was well worth it because it was a very popular event, as it is today.'

What are your earliest memories of the Show?

'I went every year. I just enjoyed going to the Show and going to the fairground and spending what little bit of pocket money I'd got on Jonty Brinkley and his wife, and going on all the roundabouts, and swings and things. And of course the other big event for young people was the grand display of fireworks about nine o'clock at night.'

Did you ever enter any of the events?

'Yes, my father insisted that I should, at a very early age – I must have been under ten – that I should enter for a gymkhana event. And that I did. For some reason or another, I don't think there was any preferential treatment because my father wasn't a judge, but I seem to remember winning a cup.'

(Richard Woodfield)

'**Kingston** Show. Well, that was a very exciting day for us because we saw all the preparation. We came back from school in the holidays just before the Show, and it really was a very big affair. My father [3rd Lord Belper] took a great interest in it, and we used to have a lot of people come and stay with us for the Show. And I remember there were a lot of donkeys there that we used to have rides on, and the house party would go down and we would all get on a donkey and have races. That was great fun! It was really quite a good show, big flower tent, all the usual side shows, and a big ring where they had the horses and cattle.'

'I was in the Coldstream Guards and I managed to arrange for the Guards to come – there was always a band invited to come and play for the Show. And the Coldstream Guards, very, very smart, came and sort of counter-marched in the ring, and then they had the bandstand up on the upper terrace. And I remember there was a man called Douglas Pope who was the director of music, and I stood and watched him conducting the band. I think it was something called 12th Street Rag. They were playing a very racy tune, and I said to him, "Do you think that I could have a go at conducting a band, it would be rather fun?" I think we'd both had one or two drinks at lunch beforehand. It was in the afternoon, and he said, "Oh yes, rather." So we went into the Hall and changed. He had a suitcase and his mufti and I put on all his regalia, then marched out without saying anything to anybody, got on the rostrum, and we did the 12th Street Rag. One of the band majors he helped me, prompted me what to do, so I was very excited, and threw my arms all over the place waving the baton around. When I'd finished there was good applause and I got down and one woman rushed up, flung her arms round me, and said, "You were much better than the other conductor," which I thought was rather a joke. The director of music, Pope, looked rather sour!'

(The Hon. Peter Strutt)

The Show in 1953

'**I can't** remember actually when I <u>didn't</u> go to Kingston Show. It was just one of the things we did every year… it was in the same category as either birthdays or Christmas - a real highlight of the year.
 The preparation was always on the Sunday. Mother used to bake bacon & egg pies, meat pasties, jam tarts, and the cake to take with us, and Sunday clothes were put out. I always wore plimsolls, which were whitened and all ready, then it was early to bed to get a good start the next morning.'

'We started early, through Long Eaton Market Place, which was always so unusual, it was so quiet in the early morning. Then down to the canal, along the footpath till we got to Trent Lock. There was a ferryman, he took us over [the Trent]. We always had a little rest there, a little cake or drink, or something before we continued on. The next stop was when we had lunch and it was [at Red Hill] where the river Soar joined, but we had to cross over [the weir] and it was a very steep incline with the water rushing down. And that was lovely there. That was to me the best part of the journey. We used to sit and have lunch, have the pasties, and all washed down with cold tea. Everyone had cold tea then, no one had pops, and there was no cans, it was always cold sweet tea. Then we walked on [from Ratcliffe] till we came to …a little lane, but we was never far from the church; over the road and then we arrived at the showground. And that was the start of Kingston Show, when you got through the turnstile.'

' The first thing that you saw was a little fair and a few roundabouts, and there was the coconut shies and roll a pennies. Everyone seemed to have a go at the coconut shy because if you didn't have a coconut, you had a pocket full of monkey nuts which you could eat as you were going round. Then there was always the big tents and the marquees with the produce, jams, and cakes from all the villages. And the big show ring… that was the centre for the big parade in the afternoon when all the winners of the different classes was parading.'

I believe you met the third Lord Belper once?

' That was one of the most memorable occasions. At that time you could go almost all over the Estate through the gardens…my father, who had been working on the Estate a few weeks before, painting, said, "We'll go through the kitchen garden." My mother saw him sneak a little green apple off a tree and she was giving him a good telling off, and he just said, "Oh well, Lord Belper said I could have an apple any time I wanted." None of us believed him, and we just sort of sniggered a bit. Anyway, a few moments after this, a tall fellow came striding down the path towards us in a light-brown suit and a – ooh, a lovely bowler, chocolate brown little bowler hat. I'd never seen a brown one before, only black, and as soon as he saw my father, "Oh, good afternoon Charles," and my father said "Good afternoon Sir." And he just tipped his hat to mother and strode off. We were amazed, because it was Lord Belper you see. So after that father walked round with a right smug smile on his face – all afternoon!'

'At Long Eaton green the Bartons buses ran every ten minutes, both ways, to and from the Show. There was always a big queue, because it was so popular. But it was very convenient because it took you right to the little green in Kingston.
 Carol, my daughter always liked to sit on the front seat of the top deck. But we was the first on the bus and [on this occasion] decided we'd sit down stairs, thank goodness. So when we got to the canal bridge [at Kegworth] there was a notice saying double-deckers this way (straight on via the bull farm) and another arrow pointing to go left for the single-deckers under the railway bridge. But this must have been a new driver. He turned left. So Tom, my husband got straight up, ran, bang – the glass divided us then you know, from the driver. In those days they were in a little cabin apart from the passengers. Banging on the door, and the driver wouldn't take any notice, and he kept going. It was only a short distance down the lane and then another gentleman joined in, but he wouldn't take any notice. Straight under the bridge, and it [the top of the bus] rolled back like a tin can. There was glass everywhere! A few boys who were sitting at the front had to be taken with cuts to the hospital, but nothing serious, apart from the bus, which didn't matter.'

Tom and Kath Garner at the Show -1959

'We never went by car. There were no cars at all, not in the early years…eventually the front lawn used to be absolutely covered in cars.'

I understand you witnessed a car accident at the Show?

'It was late afternoon… it was a very steep incline the lawn, and someone shouted, and we saw this car careering down – we just fortunately had gone over from the path where it came down. The brakes had failed or jumped off or something. And it did knock one gentleman over and it killed him, which spoilt the afternoon.'

'Every year there was one star attraction, which you always used to have to pay a few extra pennies. The one I remember the most vividly was a giant ox, and it was worth it. Because, I can always see him in my mind's eye, he was cream. Oh, and he was huge. His name? Tony. I always remember Tony, he was lovely. And they did have the biggest St Bernards dog one year as well. But they always had just something extra. I think they were more or less attached to the fairground, sort of travelling.'
'There was a fire-eater once…and a sword swallower…and then the man they always padlocked in chains. The escapologist, you always wanted to help him. There were big padlocks that everyone was invited out of the audience to lock and put round [him]. He did struggle to get out.

He used to go purple I remember. And I really didn't enjoy that.'

'I remember quite well in the Show Ring, the hunt. I don't know whether it was the Quorn or the South Notts, but they always had scarlet coats and the dogs, and they always blew the hunting horn as they went round the ring. That was one of the attractions of the afternoon.'

'I enjoyed the whole show. The flowers were beautiful , and then they got the W.I. tent. As I got older I was more interested in the jams and cakes. And if I saw anyone who I only remotely knew had won, you felt a glow of satisfaction yourself. It was a little bit of shared glory somehow.'

(Kath Garner nee Smith)

Winning display of produce – 1934 Show

'**Me** grandad were a big show man and he used to win no end of prizes with vegetables and that. In our front room on the Sunday you couldn't get in there for vegetables and flowers and one thing or another.'

' Well there was a class for children for taking wild flowers in you see, and me granddad used to say, "Get a bag, get a vase of wildflowers, put 'em in a jam jar, take 'em in. Then you get in for nothing. It doesn't matter whether you show 'em, or throw 'em away when you get in. As long as you get in for nothing." Aye, it were a great day. And the people that came you know, I mean we had about twenty five thousand folks I think it was, at the end of the day. But after me granddad died in 1936 we didn't do any more showing. Me dad wouldn't continue it.'

'The old fair used to come every year and the donkeys - the donkeys used to come a day or two before the Show, and they used to park down Miss Beeby's meadow on the Kegworth Road there. And they tell the tale that me grandad went to the pub one night, to The Anchor at Kegworth, and of course there's a footpath straight across those fields. He'd had that much to drink one night, this donkey lay on the footpath, and he fell over the top of this ere donkey!'

'After the Show we used to go with bags... paper picking. I think we used to get about a penny a bag or something like that.'

(Ron Temple)

'**At** Kingston Show when I was 10 or 11 [in 1924-25] there was a White Elephant stall, and there was this doll's house. It was from the Belper's – Strutt's – and it cost me 9d [4p]. Then I'd got to get it home, and my dad had to give a couple of Kingston lads – to bring it home on their barrow – I think he had to give them 6d [2½p] or something like that to bring it home.'

' I had that doll's house for years, and of course when I was married and had got a child of my own, I could have done with that. I'd given it away. I gave it to the little girl next door when we were at Kingston Fields , when I was leaving – I gave it to her, and of course I had to make one out of orange boxes for Barbara [my daughter]. She never did have a proper one!'

(Muriel Allen nee Brownlow)

'**We** always went to Kingston Show the night before. Every Sunday night for years we went round all the things because my dad [William Marshall] used to show cows, and of course everybody was getting things ready you see. We used to go to the Show early in the morning over that little stile towards the lake. We used to go over there and get in for nothing, then come out and get your stamp.'

' I won a prize or two for knitting and handicrafts. We used to make wool rugs for Mr Woodfield and I think Lady Belper. We used to make them at school and put them in Kingston Show.'

(Ethel Cook nee Marshall)

'The Show was held in Kingston front park with the Kingston Hall as a back drop, and wonderful terraces where we used to have the Guards bands and the Black Diamond bands. Oh, it was wonderful! We had great shows in the ring, and when we came here in 1943 - the first Show after the war was in '47 - I was elected as joint secretary with Harry Woodfield. I was also elected as the chief steward and Show manager. I built up the Show each year and it was very interesting, and the Show grew and grew until we had about twenty four thousand people on a one day show. Of course in the olden days they used to come by train to Kegworth Station and then walk down to the Show. After that, Barton's buses used to bring them. After that, they came in their cars, and the cars got so popular that we had to keep on opening fields to make more car parks. And every show finished off with a firework display in the evening for which we charged nothing. But a lot of people came, and it was most enjoyable. It was a wonderful day for Kingston. The Kingston people of course were being very crafty. Most of them went into the show grounds before the gates were open and got in for nothing, and were there all day and they thoroughly enjoyed it. Good luck to them!'

PM Harold Macmillan & Show Sec. Norman Beeby - 1963

Why do you think Kingston Show was so successful?

'Oh, because it had such a variety of interests. There was something there for everybody. I mean if you tried to itemise all the things they had, it would take a sheet of foolscap. We had agricultural implements, we had a fun fair, we had dodgems and donkeys, we had show jumping, we had cattle, we had horse classes, we had sheep classes, we had a very big horticultural section, we had a Women's Institute section, we had a bee section, we had a pigeon section, we had goats, we had steam engines. And all these things were of interest to somebody, and so it was a real family day out.'

What personalities do you remember?

'Well, every year we had a president…a very high standing president. We had the Duke of Devonshire – he was our president one year - and he brought Mr Macmillan with him who was the Prime Minister of England at the time. And Mr Macmillan gave the cups away to the prize winners. That was very good. Another one was Sir Charles Buchanan from Sutton Bonington. And we had Sir Miles Graham, we had the Earl of Lanesborough; all these in different years you understand. We had Martin Redmayne, who was a Member of Parliament; we had the Duke of Portland; we had the Duke and Duchess of Norfolk in different years, and we had Lord Trent. All these were different personalities we had each year and they were very welcome, and took a keen interest in the Show. But the great person with the Show was the 3rd Lord Belper who was extremely interested in it. Great encouragement. The great thing about Lord Belper was that the day after the Show, he went to Scotland out of the way, and we were able to clear the park up.'

'We used to have show jumping, and International show jumpers like Pat Smythe and Ted Williams, and others. Pat Smythe had a nasty fall one day and was knocked unconscious and taken to Nottingham Hospital. She housed her horses at Kingston Hall, in the stables there, for the Show, and then took them away afterwards. When the Show was closed down, she bought all the jumps that we had and they all went to Pat Smythe for her at home.'

(Norman Beeby)

Pat Smythe at the 1963 Show

'**Well**, my memories of Kingston Show as a young lad, and up to more or less the time when I got married, it were very good. We used to go down, a gang - me and the lads, and we'd try and help anybody who were trying to put anything up in the old showground, cos we allus used to get in and help them like – stall holders.'

' Then when the main day come, we used to go down, cos me father allus used to be the exhibitor for the vegetable side of things. It was a wonderful day. It were Kingston's day of glory.'

' Me father and his vegetables – he did take the majority of the firsts and seconds wi his onions, and his vegetable lay-out of parsnips, carrots and potatoes. Quite a number of years on the run, he took firsts. He took a big pride in his gardening.'

'They allus used to have something going off in the arena. I'm not sure which year, but the display was parachutists jumping out of an aeroplane. [They] jumped out over Kegworth, and I think one actually got back to the arena, but one landed in Kingston churchyard!'

(George Vickers)

'**Besides** the animals, and later in the day the fireworks, my memories of Kingston Show are of "The Produce Tent." It was a huge tent with a section at the far end divided off – this was sometimes referred to as "Muzzy Stafford's kitchen". My mother was there all day, at first supplying a drinks and rest area for the people working in the tent – Judges, Stewards, students – but over the years it became a real meeting place for old students, friends as well as helpers. It was a very early start to the day for our family. Mother ordered loaves of freshly baked bread and we made piles of sandwiches (no sliced bread or easy spread butter in those days). They were wrapped and packed into boxes ready to go to the Show. Len Price used to come and pick us up – Len drove one of the Dairy lorries.'

'Dad of course had already gone to help set up tables and make sure everything was spick and span (he was a stickler for cleanliness). The public were not allowed into the tent until after the judging and all the prize cards were in place. There were students demonstrating butter-making supervised by Miss Annie Pritchard.

' Other people I remember were Percy Walker, and a Mr.Reg Scott. Also, Bertie Shaw, who had honey on display and talked to people about his bees. The Poultry Dept. also had a display - used to love brown eggs. It was an exciting time for me, hard work for a lot of folk, but a happy time was had by all, catching up with friends and sharing mothers wonderful food!'

(Doris Henson nee Stafford)

'**It** was a great day for the village when we had the Show. A lot of traffic! Father [Angus MacRae] was usually involved prior to the show setting up the rings for the show jumping and the animals being paraded round. He and Jack Bent they used to go round and put all the ropes up for the rings for the show jumping , and have the job of collecting all the litter after the show. Father also used to exhibit vegetables at the Show. He won prizes, yes. He used to have some good carrots, potatoes and onions. I used to make cakes and exhibit those and also won prizes.'

(Ann MacRae)

Kingston Show- 1937

'**When** we used to live at Sutton Bonington, when I was a child, we used to walk to Kingston, and all we could do was look over the wall. We couldn't afford to come in. But when I started courting and came down to [live at] Kingston, we used to go to Kingston Show every year then, wait for the fireworks, and really enjoy it.'

Did you ever enter anything in any of the categories?

'Well, while we belonged to the Women's Institute, we did [enter] the cookery…I made a square cake and my daughter Valerie iced it. It was supposed to represent a basket with a lid up, and we had fresh raspberries sort of falling out of it…and we did get – the Institute did get – first prize for that. There was quite a few rude remarks…other people seeing it, saying "It hadn't ought to be allowed for professionals to enter into these competitions." But I can assure you that was about the first thing that we'd ever made, and it won first prize.'

(Vera G Smith)

'**My** mother [Grace Spiby] regularly visited relatives in Sutton Bonington, and on this particular occasion – I think it took place in the early 1930s – she had invited her sister to come with her as it was the time of Kingston Show.

It was a big occasion for them both, and definitely a time to dress up. They both had new dresses to go in, but couldn't afford new hats as well, so they decided to dye their hats to co-ordinate with their new frocks. My mother's hat was deep violet to go with her lavender dress.

The day of the show was a lovely sunny one, and off they went feeling very glamorous. Everything was going fine until the heavens opened, and there was a terrific thunderstorm. They ran for cover but the damage was done. My mother looked at my aunt and my aunt looked at my mother. Their beautiful hats were ruined, and to make matters worse the dye was running down their faces. They were so upset they left as soon as the rain had stopped, hoping as few people as possible had seen them!

This particular Show made a big impression on my mum... even right up to the time of her death at the age of ninety seven, mention Kingston, and out would come the dreadful story of the ruined hats.'

(Kate Flynn nee Spiby)

' **I went** to Kingston Show every year. I used to go with me dad for a start when he was showing the cows, and then in the later years I used to go on me own. I think the year that the Show finished, or the year previous to that, I won the Tractor Backing competition, and what's called the Loader competition, where we used to have to lift a can of milk up on the front end of the loader and place it on a trailer. I won them both....and somewhere I've got certificates to prove that. John Howick of Gotham organised it.'

(Paul Winson)

' **Father** (Len Price) filled the milk churns with water at Sutton College to take to the Show. He put them in a circle in the back of his lorry, then gathered up me, and the neighbouring children, and put us in the middle of the churns. When we went through the gate into the Show he would bang on the side and shout, "Shush"- so that we would be quiet. And we all got in for free!

After the Show he would load all the cheeses that had been exhibited, onto the lorry. The cheeses used to get hot and sweaty with the heat, (there was no refrigeration) and he took them to the College to be put down the cellar. People would try to buy the cheeses and it was my job to look after them and guard the lorry.'

(Elaine Price)

'**It was** always a red-letter day in the year to go to Kingston Show. I can remember all the crowds there, people coming from off the Nottingham train, coming down from Kegworth Station - it was just a solid mass of people. All the buses used to come down the lane. There used to be posts up to tell you where to queue for the different buses. They just ran a shuttle service as long as anybody wanted to come to Kingston.

I remember my mother telling me once - I think it was 1922 - they didn't have the Show because the ground was flooded on the Sunday. She said the beer barrels went rolling down the street, and I think the buses came on the Monday and just turned round and went back again.'

' I remember she said there was one Show, I think that would be before the First World War, when Lord Belper died just before the Show. And she said they still had the Show but they didn't have a band that year because he lay dead in the Hall.'

(Jean Spencer)

' **There** was a lot going on, because there was a fair as well. We had different tents. I remember the cheese tent very well. Then we had the flower tent, and John and I used to enter the Wild Flower competition every year. He came first, and I used to come second.

I remember the fireworks really well at the end. Everyone would wait, it had to be dark didn't it for the fireworks...those with cars would be hooting their horns. There was such anticipation built up for these fireworks...big rockets, and they had a really good display. And the Show – because it was an agricultural show - there was all the various exhibits. There was a beer tent, not that I went in there of course. Yes, it was a really big occasion in Kingston. Very enjoyable.'

(Carole Easom nee Taylor)

'**My** favourite event at the Show was the firework display, which used to close it, and I can still see now those bright fluorescent colours. They would burn behind some of the major trees in the park, the oaks and elms silhouetted against these lovely fierce colours. After all the incidental fireworks they always had a sort of finale piece. Whether or not it was Coronation year – which was the year I was seven – there was a display of the Queen and Prince Philip with the date underneath. Just thinking how beautiful it was…I can still see it in my mind's eye, right to the point when it starts to disintegrate and fade into the night.'

(Maureen May nee Winson)

Why did Kingston Show have to finish?

'**Well,** in a sense it was unfortunate, although I don't think Kingston Show would survive today. But it folded up when we had the fourth Lord Belper, Ronald. That was because there was a certain amount of damage done by some hooligans at the Show. Lord Belper saw a lot of litter there the next day, which he didn't like to see. Eventually he wanted some rent for the park, which we had never ever paid. An Agricultural Show, financially, has a job to survive, and so a rent would have absolutely killed it. We looked round for other sites but we never found a suitable one, so it closed down.'

(Norman Beeby)

Champion Shire Horse - 1963

Parade in Main Ring from the Terrace 1963

Village Shops & Trades

'if we were well off we used to go and buy gobstoppers'

Kingston's original Post Office started in 1848 at William Smith's provisions shop at No 6, Kegworth Road. By 1860 the Post Office separated and moved to No 1, The Green. The shop was run by the Henderson's from about 1920 and it later combined (at No.6) with the Post Office after postmaster Henson left. Cox's kept the shop and Post Office throughout WWII. In the early 1950's the Post Office separated again, first to No 7, The Green, and then to No 9. Eventually it moved back as combined shop/post office to No 6, Kegworth Road, where it remained until its closure in Nov.1988.

Over the years the village has also been served by both resident and travelling tradesmen.

'**I think** we were quite fortunate because we had a shop in the village. Old Edie Cox ran it.

Then we had a Post Office. Tom Henson run that when I were a lad, and of course it was only Tom Henson at the Post Office with a phone. Nobody else in the houses or the cottages had got phones in them days. I can always remember when me sister had her daughter, they rung up the Post Office to ask him if he'd deliver this message, and he delivered it. But if he delivered you any message he always used to charge you a penny delivery. And we also had a cobbler, which was George Baxter, which everybody used to take their boots there. And old George would sit in the house cobbling away.'

'We also had a blacksmith, Edmund Hall. If he wasn't in the blacksmith's shop he'd be in the pub. He was a character all right. He used to have a waistcoat, you know, with a big watch chain across him. If you couldn't find him in the blacksmith's shop when you went up - you know Miss Beeby used to let us take the horses up some Saturday mornings - if you couldn't find him there, you'd have to knock on the pub door and say, "Is Mr Hall there please?" And he'd be in there having his ale.'

'Edmund closed the shop because he hadn't got the shoeing to do during the War. You see, the horses went. Not a lot about then. So then we went from there to Harry Prichards blacksmiths shop at Sutton Bonington. Edmund went as a blacksmith at the Brush, [in Loughborough] and stayed there then till he retired.'

' We had the Co-op three times a week with bread, and we had the butchers – Shepherds of Kegworth. There were Haywoods of Sutton used to come about three times a week. Old Pepper used to come on Friday with his hardware van every week. There was an old boy used to come round with a pony and dray selling pots on it from Long Eaton. Old Atkins from Kegworth, he were a greengrocer. He used to come round with a pony and trap/float.'

' And the milk - well when I were a lad of course Jackson's were milking. Miss Jackson had got two or three cows then, at The Bungalow as you're going out (of Kingston) - and we used to fetch the milk from her every day. And you daren't smile or anything when you went, or else old Lucy used to think you were taking the 'mickey' out of her. So you had to look glum in the face. And when they finished, we had it from the milkman whoever was delivering round Kingston. But when I went on the farm you see, we were allowed milk. Used to take a can you know, a milk can, and have it from there. Then of course the College closed the dairy down so we all had to depend on the milkman from whoever was delivering it.

(Ron Temple)

'**I used** to go down with nanny or my mother sometimes to the village shop, which was always a treat, because like all children, we wanted any chocolate that was going. And there was a small shop run by somebody called Mrs Cox. My mother and nanny and her, used to talk for ages, and we used to get bored then, but we would run out on the road. In those days there were not very many cars about, so it was quite safe. We also went to the post office, and I remember I was taught to be thrifty. We used to put money into some savings account. Once a week I'd go down and put in something like a shilling (5p) or two shillings into the savings account, and that was with Mr and Mrs Henson.'

' There was also another very nice man I remember, a blacksmith, he wasn't employed by my parents. I think it was Ted Hall. He had the place at Kegworth Station [Hotel] where they shoed the horses, and so on. Of course that was a big business then, rather like garages are today. It was before the war, in the 1930s.'

(Hon.Peter Strutt)

'**A friend** and I, we used to go to church, and there was a lovely little shop just near the church. We used to get our stamps and things there, and if we were well off we used to go and buy gobstoppers. I can remember ever so well, we thought these gobstoppers were wonderful from that little village shop.'

(Nancy Speed)

Four generations of Hendersons outside Kingston shop during WWII – (Shopkeeper Edith Cox nee Henderson is standing right)

'**Well** Mrs Cox used to keep the shop, the first shop near the Village Hall. We used to call in there for like a penny's worth of sweets, and of course when we had to have the coupons, we could only go there when we'd got enough coupons to go and get us sweets. But my mother used to buy like a pound in weight of sweets. Whatever coupons she'd got she used to buy it all at once, and then when she got home she shared all those sweets out between the three of us. And if we ate all those sweets on that one day, then we had to wait another month before we got any more. So we used to take care of our sweets. But we knew once they'd gone, they'd gone, and that was it. I remember Mrs Cox quite well.'

' I used to have to push my children in the pram down to Kingston to go to the post office, from Melton Lane. Mrs Gibbons had opened up a post office between the three rows of cottages, along the Green towards the church. It was the left hand house in the middle row. That caught fire one year – somebody went in smoking, and fireworks caught fire. So she had a bit of a fire at the post office.'

(Dora Higgins nee Hogg)

'**I remember** they used to have sweets in those tall jars with screw tops on. I don't think there was quite the range of produce like there would be today, it was mainly sweets and cigarettes and that sort of thing. But I don't think they sold ice cream in those days, because I don't think they had the deep freezers to store it.

I know on one occasion I was allowed to buy two quarters of sweets when I was at school, and by the time I got home with the bags they were nearly empty - all the sweets had been given away.'

(Ann MacRae)

What do you remember about the mobile grocery vans that used to come down West Leake Lane?

'**Well**, they used to come from the Co-op at Kegworth. A fellow used to come on a Monday and take the grocery order, and the van came down with the bread on Monday, Wednesday and Friday. They delivered it on Wednesday and we paid for it the following Monday when he came again for the order. We paid for it so we were always like a bit of a week behind - that was the Co-op. We also had the butcher, he came down twice a week. And we also got the drapery van, I think it was somebody named Eddy Sutton that used to drive that.

Peppers, they came from Gotham. They sold groceries and mostly paraffin, because to start with we had a paraffin cooker, otherwise you'd got to use to the oven in the Yorkist fireplace to do your baking. But eventually we set up a paraffin stove with three burners, and an oven that you could put on top, and that's what I used to do my baking in.'

What about your milk deliveries when you first came down here?

'Mr Elliot used to come from a farm [Stonepit Dairy] half way to Gotham and he used to bring it in big churns, and measure it out with the measure into your jug. That's how we first started having milk, before bottles…and he used to bring eggs as well from there.'

'We used to go to the [Kingston Hall] gardens – I think they were open Tuesdays and Fridays – and Mr and Mrs Rowe used to run those. You could buy tomatoes and lettuce and all sorts of garden stuff. Used to walk across the park to the gardens, and that was a big help you know, for your fruit and vegetables.'

(Vera Smith)

'**We** were self supported with the old battery and glass 'cumulators. A fella named Jack Brown he was what they used to call the 'sparky' at that time of day with the wireless sets, and there was probably the odd television around, but they were few and far between. It used to be the old radio with the glass 'cumulator, and that was one of my jobs. I used to go up on a Saturday morning, take the glass 'cumulator up to Jack's house, well he had a shed behind the house where he used to do all his charging with the batteries. That used to be sixpence in the old money. You used to hand him sixpence, hand the old 'cumulator over, and get a new one off him, charged up. And that used to last us a week then on the wireless again.'

' We were also self supporting with the cobbler. We had our own cobbler in the village, his name was George Baxter. I'm not sure whether he was in the First World War or the Second. He was shot in the leg and he did end up with a wooden leg, 'cos as young lads we used to plague him a bit and say "Are you goin' to take your wooden leg off and give us a good hiding with it George?" He always used to take it all in good fun. Going back to the cobbling, he used to repair all the shoes in the village. So really, as a village, we weren't too bad.'

(George Vickers)

'**Uncle** George [Baxter] was wounded in the First World War in his leg, and he wasn't able to get…. he sort of shuffled around on his knees - on his kneepads - and he earned his living as a cobbler. He used to work in the kitchen. I can remember the smell of the leather and carbolic soap. I never used to like washing my hands there because I couldn't bear the smell of the carbolic soap! Then he had his leg amputated in the Second World War, and you know, was able to get around better after that, really. He had an artificial leg.'

(Jean Spencer)

'**Pepper's** used to come round - the old, big green van. It was, well, just a big super store on wheels really, for them days. I think they used to carry virtually everything and they always used to have …a big tank of paraffin. I used to take Auntie Win's can and fill it up for her. Also they used to have the battery man come round as well, he used to charge batteries up. Auntie Win used to have those – that was for the radios.'

(Paul Winson)

Postmistress Jennifer Hutchinson, just before closure – November 1988

Bonington was runner up, and I was the winner. We had a lovely evening the night it was announced.'

Can you tell us why the post office closed?

'Well it was mainly that the business was being withdrawn from the Post Office. So it was getting as it wasn't worth while doing it. And of course supermarkets took over from the village corner shop. Everything just went down, and it just wasn't worth carrying on, not to get in debt. So I thought that was the best thing to do.'

(Jennifer Hutchinson)

'**My** mother Winifred Brown took over the post office in Kingston in 1956. When I first left school I went to work in Loughborough, and then I came back and was with my mum in the post office. It was quite busy. There always seemed enough work for two of us.

I was post mistress when I was 21, and I was the youngest postmistress in the country at the time. I did seven years with my mum, and the rest of it I was the post mistress by myself.'

I believe the post office was once held up?

'I think it was 1967. These two youths came in with helmets on – crash helmets on – and they asked for strawberry jam. While I got the strawberry jam I was hit on top of the head. Then they came round the counter and took the money.

I had to have four stitches in my head, which Dr.Howard did. He wouldn't let me go to hospital. He came and looked after me, he was very good. I think it was the Co-op milkman who got the biggest shock when I went outside, and I just collapsed in his arms, and he got covered in blood!

But they never did catch them.'

You won an award in 1987?

'Village Postmistress of the Year. I was nominated by Renata Williams. They then came from the Post Office and interviewed me. They came round and looked, to see if everything was in order, interviewed me, then they voted on who they thought should get it. Ron Beer of Sutton

Jennifer Hutchinson outside Post Office – 1988

(Photographs courtesy of Loughborough Echo)

Village Life

'me grandad used to keep pigs'

Charles Temple and his son Ronald, back of Long Row Cottages - 1930

'**I was** born on Long Row, Kingston, in 1928. They were just ordinary cottages. There were seven there then; George Daykin in the bottom [nearest the road], Edie Smith, Mr Walster, then us, then Mr Toms, Mrs Fern, and then Mary Bramley.

Some had different numbers of bedrooms – Daykins had two, Edie Smith had one, Walsters had one, we had two, Tom's had one, Fern had one, and Bramley's three.

In our house there was a big beam went across, with a big hook so you could hang the pig on it. Me grandad used to keep pigs, and he used to kill 'em. And me Aunt Beat used to catch the blood to make the black puddings. Me granddad said there were only one waste in a pig, and that were its squeal. And if we could catch that, we'd have that. That's the only thing we couldn't eat!'

'Edie Smith, she worked in the bothy at the Hall, looking after the gardeners. Mary Bramley worked there in the first place, and Edie Smith took over. At that time the bothy was in the stable yard. Eventually they built that one down where Reg Martin lives.

Owd Mary Bramley, she had this here cockatoo. They had a cow shed that held four cows, because it was a small holding at one time, and there was a cow shed for four cows there. Of course in my time the cows had gone, and all that was in there was Mary's cockatoo. It was about forty years old, so they say. And old Billy Thirkettle in the village was a character, he tried to make it swear. It wouldn't swear, but it would shout "Cocky wants a drink of water mother," "Where's the cat?" and all that sort of thing. Anyway, she went to feed it one day, and it jumped on her wrist and pecked her straight through the wrist, and it wouldn't let go. So Mary picked a bit of wood up, hit him atop of the head and killed him. She said, "That's cured him!" And that were the end of Cocky.'

' And owd Mary nearly died on the ash heap, back of the house there. We'd lost her one night and couldn't find her. Her brother didn't know where she was. My dad and them were looking for her, they never thought she was in the back there by the cow shed. And there she lay on the old ash heap. They fetched her in, and got her warm and got her into bed, but she didn't last long after that. I were only a lad. I know she always used to wear black clothes, black woolly hat and black aprons. An' she wore nothing but plimsolls - black plimsolls, summer and winter. My mother used to buy her a pair every year for Christmas.'

'Me grandad Joe Gaskin, he were a character. He used to tell me about the night he sent me Uncle Jim to the pub for some ale, and Uncle Jim stopped and had some his self. He were a long time coming back, and me grandad were getting irritated because he hadn't got his pint, so he went across the field one wintry night to find him, and he slipped off the plank and went into the dyke. Of course he couldn't walk very fast, and by the time he'd got home and back again, and Uncle Jim were back at home with the ale, me grandad's clothes had gone stiff like a board!'

' He used to be bricky at Kingston Hall, on the Estate, and he went to do some jobs for old John Hayes when he farmed at Manor Farm, West Leake. And he said to me grandad, he said, "Do you want a drink Joe?" He said, "I don't mind Mr Hayes." He said, "If you don't mind, I don't mind," and he never give him one. So he said to me, "You always want to make your mind up, boy. Either yes, or no. Never say you don't mind." And another thing he always used to tell you, "You always want to carry a knife, a piece of string and a shilling and you've always got a friend. 'Cos," he said, "You never know when you want a knife or a bit of string or a shilling." And I've always carried a knife and a bit of money and a bit of string with me ever since. Mind you, a shilling wouldn't go very far today.'

' Fred Baxter were a right owd character. He were all right, a nice chap. When I first knew him as a lad he worked for the Council looking after the roads. He used to go right from here to New Kingston, up to Kegworth Crossroads, up to as far as the bridge at Kegworth; everything was smartly kept, the grass was cut, and all he did that with was a scythe. And the roads were swept up, not like they are today - a mess. And credit due to him.'

(Ron Temple)

' **We** lived in the first house of what they call the Middle Row of Kingston, the next block along from the church. There was eleven of us in the family.

Me, and one or two more lads and gals out the village, used to put in a fair attendance to the Sunday School. Sometimes I used to go up Kingston Brook and walk round the lake on a Sunday morning – and come back when the Sunday school was over. Years later, I wished I'd put the full attendance in really, 'cos they was lovely books what you got at the end of the year, the presentation books.

One of my jobs was to take two buckets and go across to the iron man, as we called the pump, which was the only source of water we had for using in the house for the cooking and washing. It were my job every morning to fetch two pails of water before I went to school. Night-time, when I used to come back from school, I used to fetch two more pails. Another chore would be chopping sticks in the shed, ready for lighting the fire next morning.

We had a well in the back yard which me mother used to use for the actual washing of the clothes, which was the rain water out the well. We did have coppers - boiling coppers - in the wash house out the back of the house on the yard. All over the village we had these coppers. And yer used to light the fire, boil the water up in the copper in the outer shed - the wash-house - get the tin bath off the wall and carry the buckets of hot water back into the living room, in front of the fire. Two of you in the bath at a time. Then it used to be different nights, 'cos you couldn't all have a bath on the same night 'cos of boiling the copper up so many times. Which was good fun I suppose.'

Mrs Lizzie Toms, Long Row Cottages, c1933

' We used to keep rabbits down the garden, and hens and cockerels. We had a pig sty to each house and we actually did keep two pigs. We did allas used to have one for the consumption of the house. A chap used to come and salt two sides of the pig for us, and then yer used to hang your hams up in the kitchen. Me father used to send the other one to the Ministry, and the money he got from that he used to buy two small pigs for the following year. That's how the years went by; it was rotated all the time.

The feeding of the pigs - he used to buy so much meal, and the left-overs from the house was all mixed in. That was the feed for the pigs.

The hens and cockerels we kept up the garden. With me father working on the farm, on the old threshing drum - the old wheat sheaves goin' through - there used to be what they call the chaff under the threshing set, under the main drum, where the corn used to go through. Me father used to clean it out, and have so much of the chaff for the hens to scrape into, when he chucked it down in the pen for 'em.

It was all work, but it all ended up with you getting something out of it in the end. Some say the good ole days, and a good life, they do.'

'Going back before the war there was no electricity in Kingston village. The only means of cooking and lighting was gas. That was supplied from Kegworth from the old gasworks in Kegworth itself.'

' I don't think there's one tree round the village green at Kingston that I didn't climb, or any of the other lads in the village. We used to climb them like monkeys. Later years, I joined Hathern Brass Band, I was still young and in me youth. And one particular tree, a sycamore tree next to the pump, I used to climb that on a Sunday morning and sit practising with my bugle on one of the branches, up in the top of the tree. Until I got one or two complaints from some of the older people, and got chased away.'

(George Vickers)

'**One** of my neighbours on West Leake Lane had a television in 1936. He [Mr Gosling, an engineer, who formerly looked after all the equipment at the Dairy College] were quite up in that sort of thing – him, and his pal [Jack Brown], who lived in the village about a mile and a half away. Before they had television, they used to talk to one another through loud speakers. Everybody knew what they were talking about, because all the district could

Mrs Emma Temple (wearing mob-cap) with Harry Walster, c1930

hear it. But I went and helped both of 'em to rig this aerial up. I didn't know what they were doing, they just wanted me muscles. I helped 'em rig this great big mast up, fifty or sixty feet I should think, and we got a picture from Crystal Palace before anybody in the district had ever saw a picture. The wind blew it down, and he found out you could get it [a picture] if you rigged a bit of aerial up in the attic, in the house.

Eventually we got a little telly, and I used to get a picture from a piece of wire netting. You could get it on a bit of copper wire fastened down the stair-well, before you had this fancy stuff on the roofs.'

'We had candles for lighting, and there were no piped water when we first came [1928]. We had to fetch that from a pump in the garden four doors away, until that got contaminated. Then we had to fetch it from across the field at the farm. Then they put pipes in from a tank on the hill, and that were piped down to all the people in the Lane, from this one reservoir. It used to come from Nottingham that water did, through Gotham, and supply them, and we had the end of the line.

There was a pump over the sink for the soft water off the houses. That was for washing, you couldn't use it for cooking or anything like that. Pans for toilets.

When they altered these houses - see this was the hostel for the College, the students used to live here ..there was water supplied to each bedroom - well they took all that out. There were electric lights, and they took all that lot out, and [eventually] put one light in for the whole house, stripped the wiring, everything out. Instead of flush toilets across the yard, which were there, they took them out and put pans in, which we had to dig into the garden periodically. Very basic. It showed you what they thought of the lower class didn't it? They should have left that. It were a good system. Well, it were really modern in its day.

The big shed on the ground that we had with this house, there was a engine and a pump for pumping the water from a well in the shed. And a windmill, when there was enough wind on to work the windmill. When the wind dropped it started the pump up you know, the engine up. That was all taken out.'

(George Smith)

'We went to live at Kingston Fields – it would be about 1940. I used to take milk to different homes round New Kingston. Mrs Dolman's, Mrs Hutchinson's…and I used to take the Rectory milk for so long, But I always took 'top' Evan Joyce's milk [Arthur Evan Joyce at Whitehill Farm]. Right up into the woods. I used to take bread on a Monday with the milk, and on the Wednesday I would take probably the meat that had been left at me mother's. Then on a Friday I used to have to take bread up again, as well as the milk. My mother used to do Mrs Joyce's washing. I'd bring one lot of the washing down to do, and take the clean washing back. So I used to have a big bag strapped on the back of me bike, a bag on the front of me bike, and two cans of milk on the handlebars.

I used to go of course in the winter, all weathers, delivering this milk. But to keep myself company, and so I wouldn't be frightened, I used to sing at the top of my voice. People used to say, "There's little Dora going. She's delivering the milk."

(Dora Higgins nee Hogg)

'My memories of Kingston were either visiting the allotments on Kegworth Road (now built on) where my grandfather Walster had an allotment, or trips to clip the graves of George Toms or George Walster (un-marked). Water came from the pump.

I recall visiting Mrs Temple frequently at Long Row with my mother. She used to chat, and I used to play out at the front. I recall the round cobble stones set into the ground, the small rooms, Mrs Temple blacking the range in the living room (she wore a bonnet to keep her hair clean), horse brasses (genuine of course), the winding staircase to upstairs (never saw further than half-way!), the immaculate front room, and the pokey kitchen cum wash-house. The small enclosure held the tin bath, and everything had to be shipshape for when Ron came home from work at the farm. Charlie was retired by then, but kept his distance during cleaning sessions, usually in the garden. The yard was covered in sparse grass, and there were chickens. You only went to the loo if you were desperate. The privy outbuilding was next to the nettle-infested fence (no going round the back of course!), and I can often remember the ordeal of sitting in there one summer's afternoon in the early 1950s, holding my breath only a few inches above the accumulated history of Kingston. It made our outside loo at Kegworth look like a palace!'

(George Toms)

Village scene - 1930

'We came to live in what was then the farm manager's cottage at Church Farm. We had no mains water, and had to catch the water off the roof into a cistern underneath. We had to fetch the drinking water from a pump in the neighbours garden - which we shared with the school and the schoolhouse. The sanitary arrangements were not wonderful. The bath was in the kitchen, we had to boil the copper up. The bath had a sort of lid, which you pulled down and used as a kitchen table. Grandpa built us a loo, which you had to pull. If you pulled the chain 15 times, then you had to pump it up again. So you tried not to be last!'

(Norman & Mary Beeby)

'We used to have some nice Christmas's. Christmas got spoiled by the television. We used to have some fantastic parties. I remember, it was nothing to have about 15 of us in one house in old Long Row Cottages, at me aunty Emma's…the Temples.'

(Jennifer Hutchinson nee Brown)

'**I used** to be taken to see the church, and I remember my mother [Louise Baxter] telling me the history of the Babington monument. I remember her saying, when she was a little girl, Mr Ford the sexton used to take her up the tower with him, when he went to wind up the clock.

Another of my mother's memories, she said there was this team of hand-bell ringers - I think they performed on the Green. I suppose they probably sat under the pump or somewhere on a Sunday afternoon. And Mr Turner's dog used to go and sit with them, and howl his head off!'

(Jean Spencer)

'**We** once had a chap used to come shooting on Church Farm - down the fields towards Ratcliffe. He didn't come back one time and it was getting late, so someone went to look for him, and found he'd died down there – probably of a heart attack. We brought him back to the farm on a wheelbarrow and, as it was too late in the day to summon an ambulance in those days (1950s), he was left overnight in the tool-room, sitting in the barrow!'

(Geoff Beeby)

'**I lived** at Kingston Fields from 1948-57. It was the first house you came to through the stackyard. It was very cold, more like a barn than a house. The ceilings were that high, me mum could never afford to wallpaper 'em. Perhaps the odd wall…they were enormous. We had one big room downstairs, a big playroom at the side of it, and a kitchen where we used to have a tin bath, and a copper to warm the water up. To go upstairs, there were twenty three steps to climb, all stone stairs. Very often you'd walk upstairs at night and pass a mouse running down the other way coming at you.

We had electricity, but no inside toilet. The toilet was down the garden, which was quite a way.'

'I remember Gino and Adelma Chiasserini. He'd been a prisoner of war, apparently in the cellar just below our house. I have fond memories of Gino and Adelma. In fact I grew up with them. In the summer months, different family members would come from Loughborough and we used to have – well it was an Italian skiffle group (mandolins and fiddles) – on the lawn, and they always used to play and sing in Italian. I always used to go and sit on Gino's knee while they were playing. We always used to sit in a circle, playing and singing. It was beautiful, wonderful.'

'Winnie Middleton was what you might call in a modern day world, 'Girl Friday.' She'd attend the petrol pump, was in charge of all the hens and chickens on the farm, and different things in the dairy. On a Saturday she always used to give me thruppence to go shopping for her to Kingston.'

(Paul Winson)

Local poet Mrs Olwen James, who came to live in Kingston in 1948, wrote a poem in honour of Miss Middleton :

<u>Miss Middleton – 'Wynn'</u>

I knew of a lady they called her Wynn
She was refined, elegant, tall and slim
In the country she lived, and worked by the land
Time's when they mowed, ploughed, and reaped all by hand

When for tea they ate home-made bread, butter, cakes and jam
Breakfast was fresh eggs, and home-cured ham

Wynn worked for nobility, whom she loved and admired
After long faithful service, she now has retired
This kindly 'Lady' with old world charm
Once lived quietly, at Kingston Fields Farm

Olwen James (1922- 2002)

'**In 1938**, I was in the school choir with my three sisters – there were 10 or 12 children. Each year on Whit Sunday the choir would dress in a different colour, we would assemble at Kingston Hall, then march down to the church.

I remember the occasion that year, when they announced at the Hall that Lavinia, Duchess of Norfolk (Lord Belper's daughter) had just given birth to her first daughter.

I was a Sunday School teacher, 1945-46, at Kingston church - I helped Mrs Gibbins. Mrs Brown also helped out as we had two classes.'

(Mary Sketchley nee Marshall)

Kegworth Station - erected just inside Kingston parish - on the Midland Railway, opened in May 1840. By 1914 nearly 300 trains a day passed through. The station closed in 1968.

Kegworth Station – September 1955

'**Tommy** Brown was the head porter from about 1948, the Station Master a Mr Lane. Between them they issued the tickets. My mother, Lilian Vickers, used to help portering just after the war. Old Tom Brown used to polish his lamps. Them lamps were spotless – shone off half the platform at a time.

Quite a lot of stuff for local farmers came in by train. I remember hessian sacks of dried beet pulp and flaked maize, they stood over four feet high. We had to unload them into tractors and trailers and take them to Manor Farm in Kingston. We also had to hand-load sugar beet from the College farm into railway wagons in the Station sidings.'

' I went and got a job on the railway and the section of line I actually used to work was between Marlepit Hill, Sutton Bonington, and the signal box at Ratcliffe-on-Soar. My gangers name was Bernard Downes. There were six in the team at the time and we'd be responsible for all the maintenance on it.

We would replace any sleepers or crossing timbers that were rotten. The actual chairs that the line used to sit in, sometimes some of them used to crack, so we had to replace them. It ws more or less general maintenance, and the right cants on the line for the fast trains on the curves, and all things like that, we had the knowledge of all the lot of it, for doing those sort of jobs.

In later years when I'd been on the railway a while, I was asked if I wanted to go onto what they call fogging. I had to go to Derby to the Head Offices there to pass what you call fogging rules. The job consisted of being in a little wooden hut between the four sets of lines near Kegworth Signal Box. My actual job was if a train went by with no tail light on, I was to put three detonators on that track in case there was another train following, and alert the signal man that the train had gone by without a rear light on the back. That was the main job of fogging. But there was certainly some cold nights as well. I worked on the railway just over five years.'

(George Vickers)

'**I used** Kegworth Station frequently. I used to go once a week to Fiskerton to see my father, get on the train here, and change at Nottingham. There were still steam trains, and my son's little nose used to be glued to the window.

We left Teddy George on the train once. We went to my father's, and Stu, he was only in a pushchair. He had a little black and white panda teddy. He never went anywhere without this panda, and we left him on the train when we had to change at Trent Station. Of course when we got to Kegworth, he told the station master all about it, and he said, "I'll ring them up and see if they can put him on the train and bring it back." I had a telephone call the next morning to tell me that Teddy George was waiting on Kegworth Station. Now, Teddy went to Derby, they put him back to Trent, he was put off at Trent and changed to the Loughborough line, and he was dropped off at Kegworth. I never got to know who'd done it. We asked him (the Station Master) to thank the people at Trent, but of course the rest I had no idea who they were, but I thought that was lovely. Now would they do that now?'

(Sarah [Nelle] Dale)

'**Some** of my earliest memories are looking out of my bedroom window - I could have been no more than a toddler - and watching some of the steam trains going past. I intensely remember the diesels going past with probably half a dozen steam trains in tow, on the way to the scrap yard, which still brings a tear to my eye.

In relation to the railway, I remember one incident, looking out of my bedroom window, and there had obviously been a couple of fatalities of the cattle kind on the railway. They were busy pushing a couple of carcasses, one I think was a bull, it was brown and white, the other was a fresian cow. They were from Manor Farm, and had obviously got through onto the line and been hit by a train. And they were rolling them down the embankment.'

(Stuart Dale)

Washdays

'Mondays allus seemed to be washdays'

'On Monday you never went by anybody's house without the washing were on the line you know. Everybody did that. And the owd ladies had the mob-caps on, and the long aprons – well you never see none of that now.'

(Ron Temple)

'**I don't** know whether it was the same all over the country – Mondays allus seemed to be wash day. What I used to do, I used to have a rope on a bucket and drop that down the well, and that was another one of me chores on a Monday morning before I went to school. I used to pull the well water up, and fill the copper for me mother. Then after we'd all cleared out and gone to school, she used to light the fire in the copper and get on wi her chores.

There was washing - and on the yard we had one of the old static mangles with the wooden rollers. That was another piece of equipment for draining the water out of your clothes, to get them dry.'

(George Vickers)

'We had some neighbours once. He [Mr Flowers] came to work at the pit. He came to live next door, and they'd got an old apple tree in the front garden then – on the road side. And of course Jilly, [Flowers] she'd got a line out from the house to this apple tree stump, and all this here so-called washing – which was queer sort of washing knowing Jilly. And Lady Belper came along and ordered them to take it down as it lowered the tone of the place.'

(Vera Smith)

Norah & Mrs Emma Temple, Annie Walster, and young Ron Temple – Long Row, 1930

Do you have any memories of wash-day on Firs Farm?

'I certainly do, yes. In the scullery end of the kitchen there was a copper, and…the water was heated by fire, and whites would be boiled there. Then there was a like a wash tub with a 'dolly peg' or 'ponch' to wash the clothes, and then they had to be rinsed with a 'blue bag' and then put through the mangle – a huge, big mangle – and then hung out to dry. So it was a big day, washday. It seemed to take all day on a Monday.'

' Then there was the ironing. That was Tuesday, I remember my mum [Muriel Taylor] with the flat irons, actually on the fire, and she'd spit on them to see when they'd heated sufficiently. And she always had to iron on the kitchen table. We had a big wooden farmhouse table and she'd iron on the table, no ironing board or anything. But it was a big job.'

(Carol Easom nee Taylor)

Floods in Kingston Park - 1932

Floods

'we'd got to get the sticks up on bricks & sandbag the doors'

Floods on Station Road - 1915

'**Of** course we'd got no flood banks then you know, and you'd got to keep your eye on the flood gate. If you didn't let it down soon enough you know, it used to come that fast and it used to flood. And just inside the park down in the village - the park belonging Manor Farm - there was an elm tree stood there, a few yards from the fence. Me grandad used to have me mother walk, keep going up to this tree, to see if the water had got to there. If it had got to there, we'd got to get the sticks up on bricks and sandbag the doors. And it used to come straight across the road, and straight up owd Mary Bramley's, up the gardens, straight up back of Mary Bramley's house [on Long Row], straight through her back door, through the house into the front, through the front door, and down the front of the houses. I can remember once standing behind a board inside the house when they'd 'bricked' it up, and old lady Fern used to have a tin bath under her spouting catching the rain water, and it come floating down like a little boat, down the front of the houses.'

'We had a lot of floods then, and I heard my grandad say - I can't remember when it was - that one day it rained on Kingston Show day for twelve hours and they had to put the show off and it flooded the village.' (Note: This was 1922)

(Ron Temple)

Charles Temple, back of Long Row Cottages – 1930s

'That was exceptional, 1947. Kingston was isolated. From Sutton Bonington into Kingston, the lane was exactly solid with snow from hedge to hedge across. Coming in from Kegworth side, that was blocked off as well. So it were a day or two like that before the actual farmers and the Council cut a road through on the way out of Kingston to Sutton Bonington. They cut a single road through, cut the odd gap out in between in case you met anything else coming down and you could just sort of back into it or drive in to let someone else go through. But with me not being very old at the time I thought it were great. Out comes the sledges and dustbin lids. Whatever you'd got to sledge on at that time of day, you found something to get round on. It was just great, it was! But then come the big flood after it.'

'It was great the snow was, but a week or two later we were surrounded by water. In come the flood again and the village were floating that time. Water come through the village, round the houses, in the houses, and it was a bit of a nightmare. That was the same winter.'

(George Vickers)

'The annual floods down at Ginny's Bridge were another absolutely wonderful event. It must have been horrendous for the poor people who lived near the river, who were flooded out periodically. But the word would go around when we were at school – if it had rained for a few days somebody would come back with the message that the floods were up under the bridge - and we used to go down there. We had our wellies with us and we used to go in as far as you could with the water literally just under the lip of your wellingtons. But water being water of course, that didn't last for long and most people used to go home sloshing around with a welly full.'

(Maureen May nee Winson)

Floods at Ginny's Bridge - 1961

'There have been, I think, at least two quite bad floods. I know on one occasion water was actually running down the main street to the village. I think the Water Authority had been making some alterations near the bridge [over Kingston Brook]. When the water came up, it came over the bank and then could not get back into the brook, and it ran down the village. So, quite a few of the men from the village went out with their spades and dug away at the bank and let the water get back in, and the floods receded. The cottages in Long Row, I know they've been flooded on two occasions. Water got in the houses. But thankfully that hasn't happened now since the river bank was altered at Kegworth, although there are still occasions when we get water under the railway bridge.'

(Ann MacRae)

'Several times while we've been here we've been flooded, but the worst one as I recall was when the water came in from both sides. Normally it comes off the river Soar coming this way, but this particular time we got it both ways, and it met in the street. The reason being that Severn Trent had put a monitoring device in the brook, and this particular flood time the gate or some fencing broke away from the lake in Lord Belper's park, floated along, and got jammed up against this monitoring thing in the brook. So instead of the water going down the brook it backed in the field, and eventually came over the field through that row of houses, [Long Row] and met the water coming from the Soar the other way.'

'The water at times got pretty deep so that Mr and Mrs Drury in the end house - the single house - used their kayak and went out and went over the hedge. They could get over the hedge and paddle around in the field. It was pretty deep.'

'The Evening Post photographer was down. We remember one of the girls in the village, she was coming from Kegworth on a cycle, and of course she had to get off and walk along the path because the water was deep under the bridge. In the evening paper there was a photograph of her : "Girl struggles from work through the floods." And what happened in fact - true fact 'cause we was there - they asked her to stand in the water, lift her frock up and be struggling through the water !'

(Arthur Dale)

'**There** was a severe flood in the winter of 1947 which I cannot remember, but the earliest one I can remember was 1976. There was quite a severe flood and although it never enters the properties, nevertheless it attracts quite a crowd of people. They all seem drawn to water, to see floods and danger.

It floods most of the land, but it's a short-term flood. Within 24 hours it could have peaked and gone down again, whereby you can gain access to the land. Although the river would be quite high, the actual land soon drains again.'

Does it cause many problems for boats?

'Well, we always get problems with boats with flooding, especially if people leave boats unattended. If the ropes are too tight…they either come up on to the land and capsize when the flood waters recede…or of course, the boats flood and consequently sink. I have recollections of one or two going to the bottom of the river and having to be pumped out and craned out over the years.'

How has the Flood Prevention Scheme affected your property?

'The flood prevention scheme - that started in about 1986. Of course we had to give all our tenants notice to leave. We couldn't have any tenants. They spent millions of pounds doing it. Where we had a nice hedge along the road, that was all ripped out and replaced by an ugly brick wall. They dammed the river at both ends - here and at the other end under the bridge - and actually drained the river. Pumped it dry. And I've actually walked right down the middle of the riverbed. It surprised me how little debris there was in the river; I thought when the water was pumped out, the riverbed would be muddy and smelly and it wasn't. It's a gravel or shingle bed on the river. I think we salvaged three empty bottles and a milk crate; that's all that was in there. And I'd got visions of there being old bicycles and rubbish that people normally throw into rivers and canals, but there wasn't anything like that at all.

The actual flood scheme itself was horrendous and the land was chewed up. We lost a lot of trees that were cut down, roots were cut to trees, and the trees didn't survive. We couldn't use the property at all.

'We were compensated. Whether the compensation is ever fair for what we've lost I don't know. But I always remember my father-in-law saying that it had taken two years out of his life. And despite all the assurances from the Environment people that said, "We will replant, we will put new hedges in, we'll put new trees in," he said, "Yes, but I won't see them grow in my lifetime." And sadly he never did.'

(Adrian Strutt)

1961 Floods – looking towards Kegworth

Floods in Kingston Village – 1930s. (Henry Baxter with shovel)

Kingston Park floods - 1932

Social Life

'the booby prize was a stuffed bird'

Kingston Women's Institute Fiftieth Anniversary celebration – Village Hall, 1971
(Cutting the cake are Mrs Mary Beeby, [President] Mrs Maud Marshall, and Mrs E.Rowe.
Lady Belper, founder of Kingston W.I., is seventh from right.)

'**I was** only small when the Village Hall was being built. I think Lord Belper financed most of it. But he asked the villagers to buy some bricks in it. If I remember right, they were sixpence a brick. I don't know how many me father and mother bought, but we've got shares in the Village Hall!

Before the hall was built, social events were held in the school. We used to have the harvest suppers and whist drives and that in there. I went to one, and the Rev.Jones was the Reverend then in the parish. Mr and Mrs Dobson lived in the schoolhouse, they were caretakers of the school then. I'll always remember running old Mrs Dobson's cat under old Parson Jones' long frock he wore.'

(Ron Temple)

'**I can** remember the Village Hall being built. I was about ten, and everybody in the village did things to raise the money. Me mother made tea towels. She used to make them and sell them, and the money went towards the Village Hall. I used to cycle round West Leake, and go to Kingston and Ratcliffe getting orders. This must have been about 1936.'

(Ethel Cook nee Marshall)

'**We** used to have these weekly whist drives in the schoolroom. My dad [Marshall Brownlow] was something to do with it. I added them up after a period, and then at the end, whoever got the highest mark had the best prize. And gradually you went down.

Then we used to have perhaps a whist drive and a Dance. Well, with the Dance, they used to open it all up like – the two rooms, put chalk on the floor, and you had your dancing. Quite a lot would be at the Dance. They had a bit of a band – somebody from Kegworth came. Oh, we did have some good dances there.'

(Muriel Allen nee Brownlow)

Kingston Players when they appeared at the first County Festival Final, March 1930

The Kingston Drama Society, formed in 1930, was at one time a thriving theatrical group. Up to, and through the war years, they performed regularly in Kingston, and often in surrounding villages. They continued till about the mid-50s.

'**I think** I was probably about fourteen when I joined. I seem to remember I was usually the French maid. They were farces more than anything, the plays. But village people used to appreciate them. I used to dread it though, I wasn't much good in front of people.

I'm sure I wasn't a star, just usually the maid or something like that.'

Do you recall the names of any of the members?

'Oh yes, Percy Dolman. There was a Mr & Mrs Moss from Kegworth, I can't remember their first names.[Sam & Gladys] I think Mrs Moss was a teacher up at the Girls School near the Kegworth Station, and we often used to have rehearsals there. Jean Allen, who was the daughter of the old Butler, she was in it, and I think there was a gentleman from - he's now at Normanton-on-Soar - Mr Lewin, he's a farmer.

I was associated with it for about four or five years. This was after the war. We just performed in Kingston as far as I can remember, down in the Village Hall. Everyone seemed to appreciate the performance we put on. Oh, I was a nervous wreck by the time they'd finished!'

(Christine Whitehead nee Joyce)

Members of Kingston Drama Society – early 1950s
(From left: …., Dick Maltby, Joan Rowe, William…, Peter Hill, Andrew Boughen, John Hill, Christine Joyce, George Hill, and Reg Newsome)

Lady Belper founded the Women's Institute in Kingston - one of the first in Notts – in 1921. Meetings were held at Kingston Hall. The first secretary was Mrs H.Woodfield.

Every year, about Easter, Lady Belper, president of Kingston W.I. opened Kingston Hall gardens for her "Daffodil Party" for members of Kingston and neighbouring Institutes.

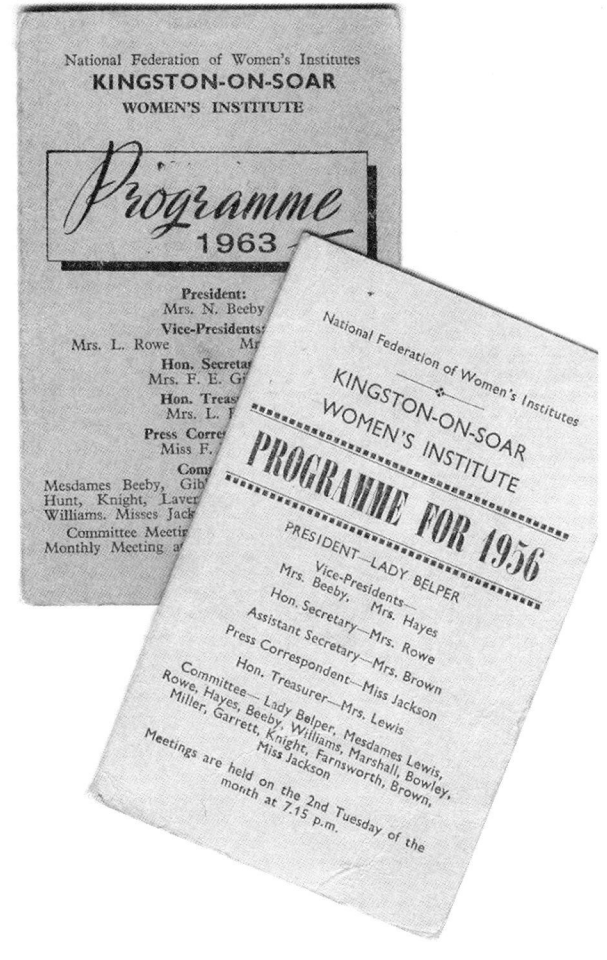

'**Always** in the spring, my mother invited a lot of people over to see the daffodils. They had a bit of a beano, tea and that sort of thing, and then they were allowed to pick the daffodils. There were masses of them. It did not make much difference to the display in the garden, because there were thousands of daffodils in the long grass. Everybody took a little bunch away with them.'

(Hon. Peter Strutt)

'**We** started off with a service at the Church and then walked up to Kingston Hall, where we picked daffodils. We were allowed a bunch of about twelve. Then we went inside for a tea party and games, usually whist. I remember once I won the booby prize which was a stuffed bird! I kept it till I left home.'

(Mary Sketchley nee Marshall)

'**I joined** the W.I. in 1943. Aunty May, who lived here, was a member and she asked me to join, and I did. I thoroughly enjoyed the W.I. Very good companions. We did a lot together, and had great fun. We formed a choir, and had a concert in the Village Hall with the Kegworth Male Voice Choir, and I got a friend to come and play the piano.

I was president for about 20 years.[from 1957] We stopped because we got down to 11 members, and it really wasn't worth a speaker coming out here. I think it was 1978.'

'I remember Lady Angela's Daffodil Parties. Although the W.I. was really non-sectarian, non-political, with Lady Belper, we always had a little church service at Kingston before we went up to the Hall.'

' The Women's Institute planted a commemorative tree outside the Village Hall in 1946, when it was our Silver Jubilee, because we were one of the very first Institutes in Nottinghamshire. We planted a second one on our Golden Jubilee.'

(Mary Beeby)

Women's Institute Tea in Village Hall – 1954
including members from Gotham, Sutton Bonington, West Leake, Thrumpton and Barton

Women's Institute members playing whist – Kingston Hall, 1954

Lady Angela's Daffodil party

Down by the Riverside

'enjoyable memories'

Riverside Bungalows, Kingston – c1935

'These six riverside chalets were built in 1932 by a Mr. Gledhill from Loughborough. They came into my wife's family in 1934, after her Grandfather had had a holiday here - I don't know whether it was a week, or a couple of weeks - and liked them so much he decided to purchase them. He bought them from Mr. Gledhill in 1934.

My wife's father was Albert Smith. He was a very well known radio and photographic dealer. He had the first radio shop in Nottingham.'

' My earliest recollection of the chalets at Kingston Lane goes back to the summer of 1947. I came with my mother, my aunt and a cousin, by train to Kegworth Station. I've got recollections of getting off the train and walking down Station Road with our luggage, which I suppose was in suitcases. I was not very old at the time, so I don't think I was carrying anything. I remember being here in the summer of '47 and going to different bungalows, and my elder cousin coming to visit. He turned up with the car midweek, probably to see that we were all right for food.

I suppose we did what people do in the country-side, we went blackberrying, and birdspotting. I can also remember in the early evening before I was put to bed, that my aunt used to buy chips from a little shop up past The Anchor, (at Kegworth) a little fish and chip shop there, which is now a house. I can't find out which [house] it was. But I remember buying a bag of chips, and we came back and fed the water rats with the chips. We'd put a chip out and the water rats would come out and eat them.'

' We've had several beasts in the river. They probably go down to the waters edge to drink, lose their footing and slip into the river. We had one a couple of years back - one that belonged to Phil Mellors over the other side of the river - the poor old cow had been in the river for quite a few hours, was getting quite upset, it was quite cold I think. In the end we got a rope around its neck, managed to make it swim across the river, and got it out on the bank the other side. Still going strong - number 53 I think that one is, according to the number stamped on its rump.'

'We had the pleasure of Olympic athlete Sebastian Coe here for two or three years. He rented no.16. That's the chalet at the far end, next to the lock. Not a lot of people know he was here, it was never publicised. He was actually in training, and I can remember him practising up and down the lawn. We've had many memorable times with him. Enjoyable times.'

'On the brook that flows alongside Kingston Lane and then into the river Soar, we had a covered boathouse across the brook. A properly built boathouse. We had two large punts in there, which is a thing you never see these days. You only seem to see them in Italy on the canals. But they used to be moored in the boathouse, and used on numerous occasions, for punt fighting and general leisure on the river.'

Punt fight on River Soar – c1950

'We have many enjoyable memories. Lots of people know the bungalows. It seems that there's always somebody you can bump into in some town, that has recollections of the bungalows, either knows of them, has picnicked there, or has had a holiday there in the past, or their grandparents rented one of them. So they are quite well known on the land. They make quite an impression.'

(Adrian Strutt)

Nottingham Radio & Electrical Social Club outing at Riverside Bungalows, Kingston – late 1940s
(Sitting centre front (light jacket) is Chairman Albert E.Smith, owner of bungalows at that time)

Interviewees

Muriel Allen nee Brownlow (b.1914) Lived in Kingston 1924-36. Now lives at Mablethorpe, Lincs.

Ethel Cook nee Marshall (b.1922, Renwick, Cumberland) Lived in Kingston 1928-32. Now lives at Kegworth, Leics.

Norman Beeby (b.1920, Bradmore, Notts) Resident in Kingston since 1943. The Beeby family have had continuous occupation of Church Farm since 1865.

Arthur Dale (b.1924, Balderton, Notts) Resident in Kingston since 1957.

Mary Beeby (b.1918, Nottingham) Wife of Norman Beeby of Church Farm. Resident since 1943.

Sarah (Nelle) Dale (b.1922, Marnham, Notts) Wife of Arthur Dale. Resident since 1957.

John Benson (b.1907, Herts.) Student at Kingston Dairy College, 1925-27 Now lives at Chatham, Kent.

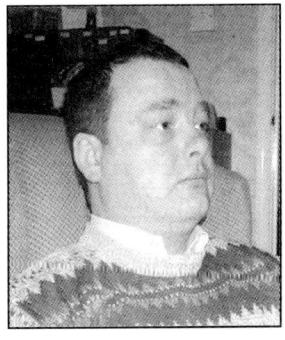
Stuart Dale (b.1962, Kingston) Son of Arthur and Nelle Dale. Resident since 1962.

Sylvia Church nee Joyce (b.Codsall, Staffs) Lived at Lodge, West Leake Lane, 1936-47; Kingston Fields, 1976-89. Now lives in Suffolk.

Carole Easom nee Taylor (b.1945, Nottingham) Lived at Firs Farm, Kingston, 1945-57. Now lives at Loughborough, Leics.

Kathleen Garner nee Smith
(b.1921, Long Eaton)
Visited Kingston Show 1920s-1965.
Now lives at Sandiacre, Derbys.

Ann MacRae
(b.1942, West Leake, Notts)
Resident in Kingston since 1950.

Dora Higgins nee Hogg
(b.1931, Gotham, Notts)
Lived at Kingston Fields, 1940-44; West Leake Lane, New Kingston, 1944- 50.
Now lives at East Leake, Notts.

Arthur Marshall
(b.1920, S.Wingfield, Derbys)
Employed on agricultural contracting and threshing in Kingston, 1940s-70s.
Lives in Kegworth, Leics.

Jennifer Hutchinson nee Brown
(b.1942, Lockington Hall, Leics)
Lived in Kingston, 1942-92.
Now lives at Kegworth, Leics.

Maureen May nee Winson
(b.1946, Draycott, Derbys)
Lived at Kingston Fields Farm, 1948-57.
Now lives at Robertsbridge, E.Sussex.

Joan Johnson nee Donnell
(b.1921, Londonderry, N.Ireland)
Lived as student at Kingston Hall, 1941-42.
Now lives at Donington, Lincs.

Ann Millard
(b.1947, County Durham)
Resident in Kingston since 1971.

Leslie Joyce
(b.1944, The Lodge, West Leake Lane, New Kingston)
Lived there 1944-84.
Now lives at Derby.

George Smith
(b.1916, Linton, Derbys)
Resident at West Leake Lane, New Kingston since 1928.

Vera Smith nee Gascoigne
(b.1915, Sutton Bonington, Notts)
Wife of George Smith.
Resident in Kingston since 1939.

Ron Temple
(b.1928, Kingston)
Resident in Kingston since 1928.

Nancy Speed
(b.1908, Legburn, Lincs)
Student at Kingston Dairy College, 1924-27.
Lives at Great Carlton, Lincs.

George Vickers
(b.1935, Kegworth, Leics)
Lived in Kingston, 1936-59.
Now lives at Ratcliffe-on-Soar, Notts.

Jean Spencer
(b.1934, Sutton Bonington, Notts)
Visited relations in Kingston since a child.
Lives at Sutton Bonington, Notts.

Christine Whitehead nee Joyce
(b. West Leake, Notts)
Lived at Lodge, West Leake Lane, New Kingston, 1936-67.
Resident in Kingston since 1975.

Adrian Strutt
(b.1944, Mapperley)
Owner of Riverside Chalets in Kingston, near Kegworth Bridge.
Lives at Hucknall, Notts.

Paul Winson
(b.1948, Patcham, Sussex)
Lived at Kingston Fields Farm, 1948-57.
Now lives at Sutton Bonington, Notts.

Hon. Peter Strutt
(b.1924, London)
Resident at Kingston Hall, 1924-53.
Now lives at Stutton, Suffolk.

Richard Woodfield
(b.1925, Kingston)
Lived at Hillside, Kingston, 1925-50.
Now lives at West Leake, Notts.

Acknowledgements.

Firstly, a special thankyou to all the interviewees. Without your contributions this book would not have been possible.

Secondly, we wish to thank the following who (a) allowed us to reproduce their photographs or artefacts in the book, (b) submitted journals, letters and diaries, or (c) helped in any other way towards the success of this project:

Muriel Allen
Geoff Beeby
Norman Beeby
Lord Belper
John Benson
J.R.Bonser
Patrick Dennis
Elizabeth Dodds (Librarian, University of Nottingham, Sutton Bonington)
Carole Easom
Kate Flynn
Kathleen Garner
Doris Henson (Victoria, Australia)
Denis Hill & Samantha Holgate-Davey (Notts. Living History Archive)
David Holmes
Olwen James
Joan Johnson
The Loughborough Echo
Arthur Marshall
Ann Millard

Gerald North
David Osborne
J.R.Pechey
Elaine Price
Mary Sketchley
Nancy Speed
Jean Spencer
Adrian Strutt
Hon.Peter Strutt
J.Talbot
Ken & Val Teare
Shirley Temple
George Toms
George Turner (New Zealand)
Susan Walker
Christine Whitehead
David Winson
Julian Wiseman (University of Nottingham)
Sue Wooley

The Authors

BRIAN WILLIAM SMITH, born West Leake Lane, Kingston-on-Soar, 8 May 1942. Attended Lady Belper's School 1947-53. After four years at Nottingham Art School (1955-59), spent 39 years with H.M.Land Registry in Nottingham. He is now retired. He has always had an interest in the history and archaeology of the area.

VERONIKA SMITH , born Nottingham, 16 August 1944. Worked in wardrobe departments of Nottingham Playhouse and Granada Television, Manchester in early 60s. Since 1976 has had keen interest in patchwork and quilting and teaches workshops and classes.

Brian and Veronika married in 1965 and have lived in Kingston since 1977. They have three children and one grandchild.

Further Reading on Kingston:

'A History of Kingston-on-Soar up to the 19th Century' - Brian W Smith, 1988

'Kingston-on-Soar: Further Chapters in the History of an Estate Village' - Brian W Smith, 1990